The Russian Camp

to August, 1915

Being the Second Volume of "Field Notes from the Russian Front"

Stanley Washburn

Alpha Editions

This edition published in 2023

ISBN : 9789357933223

Design and Setting By
Alpha Editions
www.alphaedis.com
Email - info@alphaedis.com

Contents

INTRODUCTION

MANY of my friends have urged me not to publish this, the second volume of Field Notes from the Russian Front, on the ground that the fortunes of Russia and the Russian armies were on the wane, and that the optimism which I have always felt has proved itself unfounded by the events of the past few months. It is for the very reason that conditions in Russia are momentarily unfavourable that I am glad to publish this book at this time, as a vindication of my faith and belief in the common soldiers and officers of an army with which I have been associated for nearly a year.

During the advances and successes in Galicia and Poland a year ago I found the Russian troops admirable, and now in the hour of their reverses and disappointments they are superb. I retract nothing that I have said before, and resting my faith in the justice of the cause, the unflinching character of the people, and the matchless courage of the Russian soldiers, I am glad in this moment of depression to have the chance to vindicate my own belief in their ultimate victory in the East.

The Russians for more than a year have laboured under innumerable difficulties. Without munitions, and handicapped in a hundred ways, they have held themselves intact before the relentless drives of the most efficient army in the world. Though they have fallen by the hundreds of thousands, their spirits have not been broken. The loss of Warsaw and numerous other positions has not shaken their *morale*. History will record this campaign as one in which character fought against efficient machinery, and was not found wanting. In the final issue I have never doubted that character would prevail. When the Russians get munitions and their other military needs, they will again advance, and no one who knows the Russian army doubts that within it lies the capacity to go forward when the time is ripe.

Nothing is more fallacious than to judge the outcome of this campaign by pins moved backward or forward on the map of Europe. There are great fundamental questions that lie behind the merely military aspects of the campaign; questions of morals, ethics, equity, and justice. These qualities, backed by men of tenacity, courage, and the capacity to sacrifice themselves indefinitely in their cause, are greater ultimate assets than battalions and 42-centimetre guns. That the Russians possess these assets is my belief, and with the fixed opinion that my faith is well-founded, and that the reverses of this summer are but temporary and ephemeral phases of this vast campaign, it is with equanimity and without reservation that I have authorized my publisher to send these pages to the printer.

The defects of hurriedly written copy are of course apparent in these notes, but, as in my first volume, it has seemed wiser to publish them with all their faults, than to wait until the situation has passed and news from Russia has no moral value.

STANLEY WASHBURN.

PETROGRAD, RUSSIA,
September 3, 1915.

CHAPTER I
THE FALL OF PRZEMYSL

Dated:
LWOW, GALICIA,
April 1, 1915.

I

THE news of the fall of Przemysl reached Petrograd on the morning of March 23, and the announcement was given out by the War Office at noon. The spring is very late in Russia this year, and so much snow and such intense cold have not been known so late in March for more than a hundred years. On the 23rd it was snowing heavily in Petrograd and a biting wind was sweeping through the streets. Save for an occasional street car and foot passengers the Moika and even the Nevsky Prospekt were at noon almost as empty as at midnight. And then came the announcement that the great fortress in Galicia had fallen. In an hour the news was all over the town and in spite of the inclement weather the streets were thronged with eager Russians, from Prince to Moujik, anxiously asking each other if the news which had been so long promised could really be true. The fall of Przemysl it must be remembered had been reported at least a dozen times in Petrograd before this.

There are people in as well as out of Russia, who like to say that the man in the street over here cares nothing for the war and knows less, but on this particular day these people were silent. It was no wonder. If ever a people genuinely rejoiced over good news it was the citizens of all classes of Russia's capital when it became known that Przemysl was at last in Russian hands. By three in the afternoon, crowds had organized themselves into bands, and with the Russian flag waving in front, and a portrait of the Czar carried before, dozens of bands marched through the streets chanting the deep-throated Russian National anthem; one of the most impressive hymns in the world.

Though the snow was still falling and a nipping wind blowing, thousands of the crowds that now perambulated the streets stood bareheaded in the blast as each procession passed. Old retired generals of seventy and more stood at rigid attention as the portrait of their monarch and the flag of their nation was borne past. Moujiks, princes, men and women, the aged and the young alike, displayed the same spirit of ardour and enthusiasm as each demonstration came down the street. While it is true that there is not in Russia what we in the West call public opinion, yet a stranger living here during this war comes to feel that there is growing up a spirit that is uniting all classes. This is the great hope for the war. It is also Russia's hope for the future. In another generation it is destined to bring forth greater progress and unity than the Empire of the Czar has ever known.

Occupation of Przemysl by the Russians. Austrians leaving as prisoners. The Russians entering the town.

The people of Petrograd have followed the war much more closely than one would have believed possible. Over here there has been action from the day the war started, and hardly a month when gigantic movements of some sort or other have not been under weigh. Petrograd has been called on again and again to furnish new troops, and from September until to-day there has not been a week that one could not see new troops drilling in the streets. Russia has had great successes and great setbacks, but each alike strengthens the same stubborn determination to keep pressing forward.

There was great disappointment when the Russian army withdrew a few weeks ago from East Prussia, but it began to abate when it became known that the German advance was checked. The Russians, as is their habit, had pulled themselves together, and slowly but surely were pushing back the invader just as they did in the dreary days following the Samsonov disaster in the first days of the war. Then came the news of Galicia and the greatest single success that the war has brought to any of the Allies, or for that matter to any of the belligerent powers. When the details of the numbers of the captured began to leak out, the importance of the success was first realized, and not without reason did the Russians begin to allude to the fall of Przemysl as a second Metz. It was generally believed that the garrison shut up within the fortress did not total above 50,000 men, and none were more surprised than the victors, when they learned that more than 131,000 soldiers and nearly 4,000 officers had fallen into their hands, not to mention a number of guns of all calibres amounting probably to above 300. These unfortunately have been rendered useless by the Austrians and must be charged as a heavy loss to them rather than as any direct military asset gained by the Russians.

Austrian prisoners leaving Przemysl.

Russian occupation of Przemysl. Austrian officers pay a last visit to the Russian head-quarters before leaving for Lwow.

Well may the Russians take pride in what their new army has accomplished, for one must go back to the taking of Plevna to find any such landmark in the history of Russian siege operations. The last great siege in Muscovite history was that of Port Arthur, and one cannot but contrast the state of matters in Russia ten years ago, and now. Port Arthur fell after a long series of disasters to the Russian arms, and the people all over the Empire received the tidings without interest and with that dumb resignation to disaster that is characteristic of their fatalistic temperament. A spirit of hopelessness and despondency and pessimism pervaded every class of Russian society. Announcements of new defeats were heard without surprise and almost without interest. "Of course, what do you expect?" one would hear on all sides, "Russian troops never win." But now there is quite a different point of view. Even the moujik has come to feel a pride and confidence in his army and in its victories. Their successes are his successes, and their defeats are his defeats.

One who takes interest in studying the psychology of countries comes to realize that pride of race and confidence in one's blood is the greatest asset that any nation can possess. Throughout Russia, the cause in which her Armies are engaged has come to be more nearly understood than any war she has ever engaged in. It is not true of course that the peasant knows as much as does the British Tommy; nor is there anything like the same enlightenment that prevails in the Western Armies. But in fairness to Russia she must not be judged from a Western standpoint, but compared with herself ten years ago.

As has been written by a dozen writers from Russia in the last six months the new spirit was crystallized when the war began. It has had its ups and its downs with the varying reports from the Front, but as each defeat has been turned into a stepping stone for a subsequent advance, public confidence has gradually mounted higher and higher, until, with the fall of Przemysl, we find Russian sentiment and confidence in Russia at probably the highest point that has ever been reached in the history of the Empire. The dawn of the new day of which we hear so much over here now, bears every indication of being the beginning of the much heralded new Era in this country.

II

Galicia is still under martial law, and one cannot even enter the new Russian province without a permit issued by the General Staff. It is of course even more difficult for one to get into the actual theatre of war. A wire, however, from the Staff of the Generalissimo to the powers that be in Petrograd, made the way to Przemysl possible, and a few days after the fortress had fallen the writer reached Lwow. The Russian-gauged railroad has been pushed south of the old frontier line to the town of Krasne, famous as the centre of the battle-line of Austrian defence in the days when the armies of Russky were pushing on toward Lwow.

Cossack patrol entering Przemysl.

Russian occupation of Przemysl. Governor's bodyguard entering Government House.

It was originally intended to widen the Austrian tracks to take the Russian rolling stock, so that trains might proceed direct to the capital of Galicia; but it was found that the expense of carrying on operations which meant the widening of every bridge and the strengthening of every culvert and elevated way, to take the heavier equipment, would involve time and expense scarcely less than building a new line complete. The result is that one still changes carriages some distance out of Lwow, a handicap that is trifling for passenger traffic, but involving very real inconvenience and delays in the handling of the vast amount of freight and munitions that go to supply the huge armies in the field in Galicia.

Lwow itself is no longer the dismal place that it was in the early autumn when almost every public building was a hospital, and the station a receiving depot for the thousands of fresh wounded that poured in by train-loads from the positions on the San and from the trenches before Przemysl, which was just then undergoing its first investment. Where stretchers and throngs of wounded formerly filled every available foot of ground in the huge terminus a few months ago, all is now orderly and very much as in the days before the war. The hotels which in October were filled to overflowing with officers and Red Cross nurses, are now comparatively quiet, and the city itself, barring troops going through and prisoners coming from Przemysl, is not far from normal. A few hours after arriving the writer was received by Count

Brobinsky, who frankly expressed his delight and relief at the capture of the Galician fortress.

There are of course a large number of Austrians in Galicia, and ever since the Russian occupation in September a pro-German-Austrian propaganda has been kept up here. Every reverse to the Dual Alliance has been minimized as much as possible, and every effort was subtly made by the German-Austrian agents of the enemy to prevent the peasants and that portion of the population here which sympathizes with the Russians, from co-operating in the new régime. They were assured that soon the Austrians would be coming back, and fears of reprisals when the day came have no doubt restrained a large number of Little Russians, Poles and others from openly supporting the efforts of the new government to restore Galicia to its normal state. But with each month it has become increasingly difficult for the Austrian sympathizers to make the public believe that the Russian occupation was only a temporary wave that would shortly recede. Austro-German advances in Bukowina, and the really serious aggressive attempts through the Carpathians no doubt helped to render conditions unsettled. Then came the check of the Austrian advance in Bukowina and the gradual reclaiming by the Russians of the ground lost at the first impetus of the enemy's offensive. This was followed by the failure of the relieving column to make satisfactory headway toward its objective at Przemysl.

In spite of all these very obvious failures to achieve any definite advantage over the Russians, the spirits of the anti-Russian element were kept buoyed up by the spectacle of the great fortress in Galicia still holding out. "As long as Przemysl stands out there is hope," seems to have been the general opinion of all who wished ill to the Russians. Thus the fortress, which at the outset might have been abandoned with small loss of prestige to the Austrians, gradually came to have a political as well as military significance of the most far reaching importance. In the general crash after the battle of the Grodek line, the loss of a town which until then had never been heard of in the West, outside of military circles, would have escaped anything more than passing comment. Not until the Russian armies had actually swept past its trenches and masked its forts, did the world at large know that such a place was on the map; even then the greatest interest manifested was in the vexed question as to how its name was pronounced, if indeed it could be done at all, an opinion which was held by not a few people. This place which could have been given up earlier in the war without any important sacrifice was held tenaciously and became one of the vital points of strategy in the whole campaign. An army which turned out to be a huge one, was isolated from the field armies of Austria at a time when she needed every able-bodied man that she could get; and Przemysl, which, as we see now, was doomed from the start, was allowed to assume an importance in the campaign which made its fall not only a severe military loss but a blow to the hopes of the Austrians, both at home and in Galicia. The fall of this fortress has gone further towards shattering any hopes of ultimate victory that have been entertained than anything that has occurred since the war started.

Destroyed by the Austrians before leaving Przemysl.

Principal street in Przemysl.

As Count Brobinsky, who for six months now has been straggling to readjust Galicia to the normal, said, his task has now been enormously simplified, and there is scarcely an element left here that now believes there is any chance of Austria winning back her lost province. The Austrian agents have abandoned hope, and the Russian sympathizers are now openly declaring their loyalty to the new régime. There is, however, a class of bureaucrats left here aggregating, I am informed, nearly 40,000 in number. This class is composed of Poles, Austrians and others who for generations have been holding the best offices at the disposal of the Vienna government. These are of course, almost to a man, out of their lucrative posts, and represent the element that has most vigorously, if quietly, attempted to undermine the activities of the government installed here by Russia. But even these see in the collapse of their great fortress the evaporation of their chief hopes.

As Galicia is still under martial law, all the motor cars have been taken over by the military authorities and so, even armed with passes and permits, we found it all but impossible to reach Przemysl. The best horses here are in the army service, and the few skinny horses attached to the cabs find it difficult even to stagger from the station to the hotel, and it was out of the question to go by carriage the 94 kilometres to Przemysl. But when we told Count Brobinsky of our difficulties, he solved them by promptly placing a huge military touring car at our disposal; he further paved the way for a pleasant trip to the scene of the Russian achievement by giving us a personal letter of introduction to General Atrimanov, the new Russian commandant of the captured fortress.

III

The spring is late here as it is throughout Russia this year, and it was snowing heavily as our big touring car, with a soldier as chauffeur, threaded its way in the early morning through the narrow streets of Lwow and out into the open country which was now almost white. Before we have been twenty minutes on the road we begin to pass occasional groups of dismal wretches in the blue uniform which before this war was wont to typify the might of the Hapsburgs, but which now in Galicia is the symbol of dejection and defeat. Through the falling snow they plod in little parties of from three to a dozen; evidently the rear guard of the column that went through yesterday, for they are absolutely without guards, and are no doubt simply dragging on after their regiments.

Austrian and Hungarian prisoners en route to Lwow.

From Lwow almost due west runs the line of the highway to Grodek where we get our first glimpse of prisoners in bulk. Here, at the scene of some of the fiercest fighting that the war has produced, is a rest station for the columns that are making the journey to Russian captivity on foot from Przemysl to Lwow, and I know not how far beyond. As we motor into the town the three battalions of the 9th Hungarian regiment of the 54th Landsturm brigade are just straggling into the town from the west. With a few Russians who seem to be acting as guides and nurses rather than as guards, they file through the streets and into a great square of a barracks. Here they are marshalled in columns of four, and marched past the door of the barracks where an official counts the individual fours and makes a note of the number that have passed his station. Beyond in a grove the ranks are broken, and the weary-looking men drop down under the trees, regardless of the snow and mud, and shift their burdens and gnaw at the hunks of bread and other provisions furnished them by the Russians.

It is hard to realize that the haggard despondent rabble that we see has ever been part of an actual army in being. Most of them were evidently clothed for a summer campaign, and their thin and tattered uniform overcoats must have given but scant warmth during the winter that has passed. The line is studded with civilian overcoats, and many of the prisoners have only a cap or a fragment of a uniform which identifies them as ever having been soldiers at all. The women of the village pass up and down the line giving the weary troops bits of provision not in the Russian menu. All the men are wan and thin, with dreary hopelessness written large upon their faces, and a vacant stare of utter desolation in their hollow eyes. They accept gladly what is given and make no comment. They get up and sit down as directed by their guards, apparently with no more sense of initiative or independence of will than the merest automatons. We pause but a few minutes, for the roads are bad and we are anxious to get over the muddy way as quickly as possible.

The western portion of Grodek was badly knocked up by shell fire during the battle in September, and the barren walls of charred buildings remain to tell the story of the Austrian effort to stay the tide of the Russian advance that swept them out of position after position during the first weeks of the war. Grodek was reported to have been utterly destroyed at the time, but as a fact, not more than one-fifth of the buildings were even damaged by the artillery fire.

Austrian prisoners resting by the roadside during their march from
Przemysl.

Just east of Sadowa Wisznia, the scene of another Austrian stand, we come
upon a regiment attached to the 54th Landsturm brigade. This is the tenth
regiment, and, with the exception of a few non-commissioned officers, is
composed entirely of Slovaks and Hungarians. They are resting as we motor
up, and for nearly a mile they are sitting dejectedly by the side of the road,
some with heads resting wearily against tree trunks, while dozens of others
are lying in the snow and mud apparently asleep. As nearly as I could
estimate, there is about one Russian to a hundred prisoners. In any case one
has to look about sharply to see the guards at all. It reminds one a bit of
trying to pick a queen bee out of a swarm of workers. Usually one discovers
the guard sitting with a group of prisoners, talking genially, his rifle leaning
against the trunk of a tree near by.

We stopped here for about half an hour while I walked about trying to find
some prisoners who could speak German, but for the most part that language
was unknown to them. At last I discovered a couple of non-commissioned
officers, who, when they heard that I was an American, opened up and talked
quite freely. Both took great pride in repeating the statement that Przemysl
could never have been taken by assault, and that it had only surrendered
because of lack of food.

One of the men was from Vienna and extremely pro-German in his point
of view. He took it as a matter of course that the Austrians were defeated
everywhere, but seemed to feel a confidence that could not be shaken in the
German troops. He knew nothing of the situation outside of his own

garrison, and when told of Kitchener's new British Army, laughed sardonically. "It is a joke," he said, "Kitchener's army is only on paper, and even if they had half a million as they claim to have, they would be of no use. The English cannot fight at all." When told that over two million men had been recruited in the British Empire he opened his eyes a bit, but after swallowing a few times he came back, "Well even if they have it does not matter. They can't fight."

The other man whom I questioned was mainly interested in how long the war was going to last. He did not seem to feel any particular regret at the fall of the fortress, nor to care very much who won, as long as it would soon be over so that he could go home again. As for the rank and file I think it perfectly safe to suggest that not one in a hundred has any feeling at all except that of hopeless perpetual misery. They have been driven into a war for which they care little, they have been forced to endure the hardships of a winter in the trenches with insufficient clothing, a winter terminating with a failure of food supplies that brought them all to the verge of starvation. The fall of the fortress means to them three meals of some sort a day, and treatment probably kinder than they ever got from their own officers. They are at least freed from the burden of war and relieved of the constant menace of sudden death which has been their portion since August.

The road leading west from Sadowa Wisznia is in fearful condition owing to the heavy traffic of the Russian transport, and in places the mud was a foot deep. The country here is flat with occasional patches of fir and spruce timber. It is questionable if there ever was much prosperity in this belt; and since it has been swept for six months by contending armies, one cannot feel much optimism as to what the future has in store for the unfortunate peasants whose homes are destroyed, and whose live stock is said to have been taken off by the Austrians as they fell back before the Russians.

IV

One's preconceived idea of what a modern fortress looks like vanishes rapidly as one enters Przemysl. In time of peace it is probable that a layman might pass into this town without suspecting at all that its power of resisting attack is nearly as great as any position in all Europe. Now, of course, innumerable field works, trenches, and improvised defences at once attract the attention; but other than these there is visible from the main road but one fortress, which, approached from the east is so extremely unpretentious in appearance that it is doubtful if one would give it more than a passing glance if one were not on the lookout for it.

Przemysl itself is an extremely old town which I believe was for nearly 1,000 years a Russian city. From remote days of antiquity it has been a fortress, and following the ancient tradition, each successive generation has kept improving its defences until to-day it is in reality a modern stronghold. Why the Austrians have made this city, which in itself is of no great importance, the site of their strongest position, is not in the least obvious to the layman observer. The town itself, a mixture of quaint old buildings and comparatively modern structures, lies on the east bank of the river San— which at this point is about the size of the Bow river at Calgary, in Canada— and perhaps 3 kilometres above the point where the small stream of the Wiar comes in from the south. The little city is hardly visible until one is almost upon it, so well screened is it by rolling hills that lie all about it. Probably the prevailing impression in the world has been that the Russian great guns have been dropping shells into the heart of the town; many people even in Lwow believe it to be in a half-ruined condition. As a matter of fact the nearest of the first line of forts is about 10 kilometres from the town itself, so that in the whole siege not a shell from the Russian batteries has fallen in the town itself. Probably none has actually fallen within 5 kilometres of the city. There was therefore no danger of the civilian population suffering anything from the bombardment while the outer line of forts held as they did from the beginning.

Austrian prisoners leaving Przemysl.

The only forts or works which we were given the opportunity of seeing, were those visible from the road, the authorities informing us that they had reason to believe that many of the trenches and positions were mined, and that no one would be permitted in them until they had been examined by the engineers of the army and pronounced safe. If the works seen from the road are typical of the defences, and I believe they are, one can quite well realize the impregnable nature of the whole position. The road from Lwow comes over the crest of a hill and stretches like a broad ribbon for perhaps 5 kilometres over an open plain, on the western edge of which a slight rise of ground gives the elevation necessary for the first Austrian line. To the north of the road is a fort, with the glacis so beautifully sodded that it is hardly noticeable as one approaches, though the back is dug out and galleried for heavy guns. Before this is a ditch with six rows of sunken barbed wire entanglements, and a hundred yards from this is another series of entanglements twelve rows deep, and so criss-crossed with barbed wire that it would take a man hours to cut his way through with no other opposition.

To the right of the road runs a beautifully constructed line of modern trenches. These are covered in and sodded and buried in earth deep enough to keep out anything less than a 6-inch field howitzer shell unless it came at a very abrupt angle. To shrapnel or any field gun high explosive shell, I should think it would have proved invulnerable. The trench itself lies on a slight crest with enough elevation to give loop holes command of the terrain before. The field of fire visible from these trenches is at least 4 kilometres of country, and so perfectly cleared of shelter of all sorts that it would be difficult for a rabbit to cross it unseen. The ditch and two series of wire entanglements extend in front of the entire position. This line is, I believe, typical of the whole outer line of fortifications, which is composed of a number of forts all of which are tied together with the line of trenches. The outer line is above 40 kilometres in circumference, from which it may be judged to what great expense Austria has been put in fortifying this city. I was not able to get any accurate information as to the number of guns which the Austrians have on their various positions, but the opinion of a conservative officer was, that, excluding machine guns, there were at least 300 and possibly a greater number. The inventory has not yet been completed by the Russians. These are said to range in calibre from the field piece up to heavy guns of 30 centimetres. I was informed that there were a few 36 and one or two of the famous 42 centimetres here when the war started, but that the Germans had borrowed them for their operations in the West. In any case it is hard to see how the big guns, even of the 30 centimetres, would be of any great value to a defence firing out over a crest of hills in the distant landscape behind which, in an irregular line of trenches, an enemy lay.

After a few experiments against the works, the Russians seem to have reached the conclusion that it would not be worth while even to attempt carrying the trenches by assault. Indeed, in the opinion of the writer neither the Russians nor any other troops ever could have taken them with the bayonet; the only method possible would have been the slow and patient methods of sapping and mining which was used by the Japanese at Port Arthur. But methods so costly, both in time and lives, would seem to have been hardly justified here because, as the Russians well knew, it was merely a question of time before the encircled garrison would eat itself up, and the whole position would then fall into their hands without the cost of a single life.

The strategic value of Przemysl itself was in no way acutely delaying the Russian campaigns elsewhere, and they could afford to let the Austrian General who shut himself and a huge army up in Przemysl, play their own game for them, which is exactly what happened. There was no such situation here as at Port Arthur, where the menace of a fleet in being locked up in the harbour necessitated the capture of the Far Eastern stronghold before the Russian second fleet could appear on the scene and join forces with it. Nor was there even any such important factor as that which confronted the Germans at Liège. To the amateur it seems then that the Austrians, with eyes open, isolated a force which at the start must have numbered nearly four army corps, in a position upon which their programme was not dependent, and under conditions which made its eventual capture a matter of absolute certainty providing only that the siege was not relieved from without by their own armies from the South.

The lesson of Przemysl may be a very instructive one in future wars. The friends of General Sukomlinoff, the Russian Minister of War, are claiming with some reason that what has happened here is a vindication of the Minister's theory, that fortresses in positions which are not of absolute necessity to the military situation should never be built at all, or should be abandoned at the inception of war rather than defended unwisely and at great cost. It is claimed that if the Warsaw forts had not been scrapped some years ago, the Russian Army to-day would be standing a siege, or at least a partial siege, within the city, rather than fighting on a line of battle 40 kilometres to the west of it. Port Arthur is perhaps an excellent example of the menace of a fortified position of great strength. So much had been done to make that citadel impregnable that the Russians never dreamed of giving it up. The result was that a position, which was doomed to succumb eventually, was made the centre of all the Russian strategy. For months the army in the North was forced to make attempt after attempt to relieve the position, with the results that they lost probably four times the number of the garrison in futile efforts to relieve it. A fortress which has cost large sums of money must be defended at any cost to justify the country that has incurred the expense. Forces which can probably be ill spared from field operations are locked up for the purpose of protecting expensive works which, as in the case of Przemysl, yield them little or nothing but the ultimate collapse of their defence, and the consequent demoralization of the field armies which have come to attach an importance to the fortress which, from a strategic point of view, it probably never possessed.

V

The last few kilometres of the road into Przemysl was alive with Russian transport plodding into the town, but the way was singularly free from troops of any sort. With the exception of a few Cossack patrols and an occasional officer or orderly ploughing through the mud, there was nothing to indicate that a large Russian army was in the vicinity. It is possible that it has already been moved elsewhere; in any case we saw nothing of it.

Between the outer line of forts and the Wiar river are a number of improvised field works, all of which looked as though they could stand a good bit of taking, but of course they were not as elaborate as the first line. The railroad crosses the little Wiar on a steel bridge, but the bridge now lies a tangle of steel girders in the river. It is quite obvious that the Austrian commander destroyed his bridges west of the town because they afforded direct communications with the lines beyond; but the bridge over the Wiar has no military value whatsoever, the others being gone, save to give convenient *all rail* access to the heart of Przemysl itself. The town was given up the next day and, as the natural consequence of the Austrian commander's conception of his duty, all food supplies had to be removed from the railway trucks at the bridge, loaded into wagons, and make the rest of the journey into the town in that way, resulting in an absolutely unnecessary delay in relieving the wants of the half-famished garrison within. The only bright spot that this action presents to the unprejudiced observer is that it necessitated the dainty, carefully-shod Austrian officers walking three kilometres through the mud before they could embark on the trains to take them to the points of detention for prisoners in Russia. There cannot be the slightest doubt that the rank and file of the garrison were actually on the verge of starvation, and that the civilian population were not far from the same fate. As near as one can learn the latter consisted of about 40,000 persons. I am told that the prisoners numbered 131,000 men and some 3,600 officers, and that perhaps 20,000 have died during the siege from wounds and disease. This, then, makes a population at the beginning of nearly 200,000 in a fortification which, as experts say, could have easily been held by 50,000 troops. One officer even went so far as to declare that in view of the wonderful defensive capacity of the position 30,000 might have made a desperate stand. The fortress was thus easily three times over garrisoned. In other words there were perhaps at the start 150,000 mouths to feed in the army alone, when 50,000 men would have been able to hold the position. This alone made the approach of starvation sure and swift. The fact that in this number of men there were 3,600 officers, nine of the rank of General, indicates pretty clearly the extent to which the garrison was over officered. Kusmanek, the commander of the fortress, is said to have had seventy-five officers on his personal staff alone.

As far as one can learn there was no particular pinch in the town until everything was nearly gone, and then conditions became suddenly acute. It is improbable that economy was enforced in the early dispensing of food supplies, and the husbanding of such resources as were at hand. When the crisis came, it fell first upon the unfortunate soldiers, with whom their officers seem to have little in common. Transport horses were killed first, and then the cavalry mounts went to the slaughter house to provide for the garrison. The civilians next felt the pinch of hunger, and every live thing that could nourish the human body was eaten. Cats I am told were selling at ten kr. each and fair-sized dogs at twenty-five kr. The extraordinary part of the story is that according to evidence collected from many sources the officers never even changed their standards of living. While the troops were literally starving in the trenches, the dilettantes from Vienna, who were in command, were taking life easily in the Café Sieber and the Café Elite. Three meals a day, fresh meat, wines, cigarettes and fine cigars were served to them up to the last.

One of the haggard starved-looking servants in the hotel where I was quartered told me that several of the staff officers lived at the hotel. "They," he said, "had everything as usual. Fresh meat and all the luxuries were at their disposal until the last. Yet their soldier servant used to come to me, and one day when I gave him half of a bit of bread I was eating, his hands trembled as he reached to take it from me." My informant paused and then concluded sardonically, "No, the officers did not suffer. Not they. It was cafés, billiards, dinners and an easy life for them to the end. But the rest of us. Ah, yes, we have suffered. Had the siege lasted another week we should all have been black in the face for want of food."

An Austrian sister who had been working in the hospital confirmed the story. "Is it true that people were starving here?" I asked her. "Indeed it is true," she told me, "the soldiers had almost nothing and the civilians were little better off. As for us in the hospitals—well, we really suffered for want of food." "But how about the officers?" I asked. She looked at me sharply out of the corner of her eyes, for she evidently did not care to criticize her own people, but she seemed to recall something and her face suddenly hardened as she snapped out: "The officers starve? Well, hardly. They lived like dukes always." More she would not say, but the evidence of these two was amply confirmed by the sight of the sleek well-groomed specimens of the "dukes" that promenade the streets. While the soldiers were in a desperate plight for meat, the officers seemed to have retained their own thoroughbred riding horses until the last day. I suppose that riding was a necessity to them to keep in good health. The day before the surrender they gave these up, and 2,000 beautiful horses were killed, not for meat for the starving soldiers be it noted, but that they might not fall into the hands of the Russians. Perhaps I can best illustrate what happened by quoting the words of a Russian officer who was among the first to enter the town. "Everywhere," he told me, "one saw the bodies of freshly-killed saddle horses, some of them animals that must have been worth many thousand roubles. Around the bodies were groups of Hungarian soldiers tearing at them with knives; with hands and faces dripping with blood, they were gorging themselves on the raw meat. I have never seen in all my experience of war a more horrible and pitiable spectacle than these soldiers, half crazed with hunger, tearing the carcasses like famished wolves." My friend paused and a shadow crossed his kindly face. "Yes," he said, "it was horrible. Even my Cossack orderly wept—and he—well, he has seen much of war and is not over delicate."

I can quote the statement of the Countess Elizabeth Schouvalov, of whom more anon, as further corroborative evidence of conditions existing in the town. The Countess, who is in charge of a distribution station to relieve the wants of the civil population, said to me: "It is true that the people were starving. Common soldiers occasionally fell down in the street from sheer weakness for want of food. Some lay like the dead and would not move. But their officers!" A frown passed over her handsome features. "Ah!" she said, "they are not like the Russians. Our officers share the hardships of the men. You have seen it yourself," with a glance at me, "you know that one finds them in the trenches, everywhere in uniforms as dirty as their soldiers, and living on almost the same rations. A Russian would never live in ease while his men starved. I am proud of my people. But these officers here—they care nothing for their men. You have seen them in the streets. Do they look as though they had suffered?" and she laughed bitterly.

I had not been above a few hours in Przemysl before it was quite clear to me, at least, that Przemysl surrendered for lack of food, and that while the officers were living luxuriously, their men were literally starving. That they let them starve while they kept their own pet saddle horses seems pretty well established from the evidence obtainable. One wonders what public opinion would say of officers in England, France or America who in a crisis proved capable of such conduct?

In my comments on the Austrian officers I must of course limit my observations to the types one sees, and hears about, in Przemysl. Out of 3,600 officers there must have been men of whom Austria can be proud, men who did share their men's privations, and these, of course, are excepted from the general observations.

Russian Governor of Przemysl.

VI

Immediately on reaching the town we sought out the head-quarters of the new Russian Commandant of the fortress. Over the door of the building, in large gold letters, were words indicating that the place had formerly been the head-quarters of the 10th Austrian Army Corps. At the entrance two stolid Russian sentries eyed gloomily the constant line of dapper Austrian officers that passed in and out, and who were, as we subsequently learned, assisting the Russians in their task of taking over the city. General Artimonov, the new governor, received us at once in the room that had been vacated only a few days before by his Austrian predecessor General Kusmanek. On the wall hung a great picture of the Austrian Emperor. The General placed an officer, Captain Stubatitch, at our disposal, and with him our way was made comparatively easy. From him and other officers whom we met, we gathered that the Russians were utterly taken by surprise at the sudden fall of the fortress, and dumbfounded at the strength of the garrison, which none believed would exceed the numbers of the Russians investing them; the general idea being that there were not over 50,000 soldiers at the disposal of the Austrian commander.

Three days before the fall a sortie was made by some 30,000 Hungarian troops. Why out of 130,000 men only 30,000 were allotted to this task in such a crisis does not appear. Neither has any one been able to explain why, when they did start on their ill-fated excursion, they made the attempt in the direction of Lwow rather than to the south, in which direction, not so very far away, the armies of Austria were struggling to reach them. Another remarkable feature of the last sorties was, that the troops went to the attack in their heavy marching kit. Probably not even the Austrians themselves felt any surprise that such a half-hearted and badly organized undertaking failed with a loss of 3,500 in casualties and as many more taken prisoners. One does not know how these matters are regarded in Austria, but to the laymen it would seem that some one should have a lot of explaining to do as to the last days of this siege. Officers who have been over the ground state that in view of the vast numbers of the garrison, and the fact that they were well supplied with ammunition, there would have been great chance of an important portion of the beleaguered breaking through and getting clean away to the south; but no attempt of this nature seems to have been made.

Russian occupation of Przemysl. Head-quarters of Staff.

The night before the surrender, the Austrians began destroying their military assets, and for two hours the town was shaken with the heavy explosions of bridges and war material of all sorts. Every window facing the San river was broken by the overcharge of the explosives that destroyed the bridges. Simultaneously the work of destroying the artillery was going on in all the forts with such efficiency, that it is doubtful if the Russians will get a single piece that can be used again. The soldiers even destroyed the butts of their muskets, and the authorities, who were evidently keen on this part of the work, arranged for tons of munitions to be dumped into the river. Others were assigned to kill the saddle-horses.

By daylight the task seems to have been completed and negotiations for surrender were opened by the Austrians. Our guide, Captain Stubatitch, was the first Russian to enter the town as a negotiator, and through him the meeting of ranking officers was arranged—a meeting that resulted in the unconditional surrender of the fortress. The original terms agreed on between Kusmanek and General Silivanov, the commander of the Russian forces, did not permit the Austrian officers to carry their side arms; but a telegram from the Grand Duke spared them the humiliation of giving up their swords, a delicate courtesy, which it seems to the writer was quite wasted on the supercilious Austrian officers. In the first place there has been no formal entrance of Russian troops, Silivanov himself not yet having inspected his prize. The first Russians to enter came in six military touring cars absolutely without any escort, and went quietly and unostentatiously to the head-quarters of the Austrian commander where the affairs of the town were transferred with as little friction as the changing of the administration of one defeated political party into the hands of its successor. Following the officials, small driblets of troops came in to take over sentry and other military duties, and then came the long lines of Russian transport bringing in supplies for the half-famished garrison. All told, probably there have not been above a few thousand Russian soldiers in Przemysl since its capitulation, and these were greeted warmly by both prisoners and civilians. There has been no friction whatever and everybody seems well satisfied with the end of the siege. The greatest task at first was the relief of the population, both soldiers and civilians. Countess Schouvalov, whom I have mentioned before, came the second day and immediately began feeding the population from the depôt where she organized a kitchen and service of distribution which alone takes care of 3,000 people a day. The Army authorities arranged for the care of the soldiers and much of the civil population as well, and in three days the situation was well in hand and practically all the suffering eliminated.

Feeding Austrian prisoners en route to Lwow.

I have talked with many people in Przemysl, and civilians and prisoners alike speak of the great kindness of the Russians from the ranking officers down to the privates, all of whom have shown every desire to ameliorate the distress. The difficulty of feeding so vast a throng necessitated the immediate evacuation of the prisoners, and an evacuation office was at once organized. Batches of prisoners started toward Lwow at the rate of about ten thousand a day, which is about all the stations along the route can handle conveniently with supplies. The officers are sent out in small blocks by rail once a day, and are, I believe for the most part taken directly to Kiev, where they will remain until the end of the war.

General Kusmanek himself departed the first day in a motor car to the head-quarters of Silivanov and thence with the bulk of his staff to Kiev. Those who have seen him describe him as a youngish man looking not over forty, but in reality fifty-four. A man who saw him the day of the surrender told me that he had accepted the situation very casually, and had seemed neither depressed nor mortified at the turn events had taken. The ranking officer left in Przemysl is General Hubert, formerly Chief of Staff, who is staying on to facilitate the transfer of administrations; the head-quarters is filled with a mixture of officers and orderlies of both armies working together in apparent harmony.

The fall of Przemysl strikes one as being the rarest thing possible in war— namely a defeat, which seems to please all parties interested. The Russians rejoice in a fortress captured, the Austrians at a chance to eat and rest, and the civilians, long since sick of the quarrel, at their city once more being restored to the normal.

General Hubert, Chief of Austrian Staff in Przemysl.

CHAPTER II
WARSAW IN APRIL, 1915

Dated:

WARSAW, POLAND,
May 1, 1915.

WITH the sunshine and balmy weather of the beautiful Polish spring, there has come to Warsaw an optimism and hopefulness that is deeper rooted and certainly more widely spread than the feeling of relief that swept through the city in October last when the Germans, after their futile effort to take it, began their retreat to their own frontier. On that occasion the population had barely time to get its breath, and to begin to express some optimism as to the war, when the news came that the Germans were advancing for a second time on the Polish capital.

Warsaw, as I have seen it in nearly a dozen visits here since the war began, is a little panicky in disposition, perhaps with reason; and there have been such a continuous ebb and flow of rumours good and bad, that for months no one knew what to expect. All through December and January one heard every few days that the Germans would take the town almost any time, only to be told the next day that all chances of Teuton success were forever gone. Tales of German raids, aeroplanes, Zeppelins on the way to destroy the city were circulated so persistently, that perhaps it was not strange that genuine optimism found the soil of local public opinion a difficult one in which to take root. The end of the first week of February left the public here greatly encouraged, for had not the stupendous German attack failed on the Bzura-Rawka line?

But following close on its heels came the news of the movement in East Prussia and Russian retirements, and once more confidence fled. Later still the enemy's advance on Przasnys and the threat to the Petrograd-Warsaw line made conditions even worse. This was the low-water mark. When the terrific attacks began to weaken and at last the columns of the Kaiser began to give place, conviction that the worst was over for Warsaw began to be felt generally, until to-day, May 1, I find a buoyancy and hopefulness here that I have not seen in any part of Russia since the war started.

The reasoning of the people here is something like this. In the attacks of January and February the Germans were putting into the field the best men and the most of them that they could lay their hands on, and still not weakening their position in the West. The onslaught on the Bzura-Rawka line is believed to have been one of the fiercest efforts that the Germans up to that date had made on any Front. Six corps and, as it is said, 600 guns were concentrated on a short front and almost without interruption they attacked for six days. The net result was nothing save a few unimportant dents in the Russian line, and the German loss is placed at 100,000 men. The Russians certainly did not lose half that number, and some well-informed people who have been on this Front for months think it may have been little more than a third.

The East Prussian attack and its corollary movement against Przasnys raged with the same fury. For nearly a month Poland was taking an account of stock. Now it has become the opinion of practically every one, even down to the common soldiers, that the whole German movement has proved an utter failure and at a cost to the enemy of not under 200,000, a figure from two to three times as great as was the decrease of the Russian forces. Even the East Prussian retirement which was so heralded abroad by the Germans has been gradually shrinking, until now it is said that the total loss to the Russians was only 25,000 to 30,000 against the 100,000 which the Germans claimed. "How is it possible," people say here, "for the Germans to accomplish something in May that they could not do in February?" Certainly they can never be materially stronger than they were when the first attack on the Bzura line was launched in the end of January, and the chances are that they are greatly weaker.

The Russians, on the other hand, are stronger now by a very great deal than they were on February 1st, and are getting stronger and stronger with every day that the war lasts. It is probably safe to say that there are 25 per cent. more troops on this Front to-day than there were when the Russians threw back the Germans two months ago, and the feeling that Warsaw will never be taken has become a conviction among the Poles. The rumour-mongers, and there are hundreds here who wish evil to the Russians, find it more and more difficult to start scares; and even reports of Zeppelins and air raids create little comment. So common have bombs become that the appearance of aircraft above the city creates no curiosity and very little interest. I have been especially impressed with the determination with which the Poles are planning to combat the German influence in the future. Though Poland has suffered hideously through this war, there is small cry here for peace at any price, and the opinion voiced a few days ago by one of the leading papers seems to be that of all the practical and most influential men of the community. This view was that the war must be fought out to a decisive issue, and though Poland must suffer longer thereby, yet anything short of complete success would be intolerable. While the Poles are still thinking a great deal about their political future, they are perhaps more keenly alive as to their industrial and economic future. As one well-informed individual expressed it, "With economic and industrial prosperity we may later get all we want politically. But without them mere political gains will profit us little."

A Russian officer inspecting eight-inch gun.

What the Poles want most perhaps in the final peace is a boundary line that will give Russia the mouth of the Vistula at Danzig. With an absolute freedom of trade with England, America and the outside world, Poland will have a prosperity which will go a very long way toward helping them to recuperate from the terrible blow that their nation has received in the war. That this is serious no one can doubt. Conditions within that portion of Poland occupied by the enemy are said to be deplorable beyond measure. It is difficult to know here exactly what the truth is, but it is probable that the suffering of the unfortunate peasants, who are for the most part stripped of their stock and in many instances without homes, is very severe. With the war lasting all summer and no chance for a crop, their plight by autumn will be serious. What is being done about putting in a crop for the coming year is uncertain, but it is said that there is practically no seed for sowing, and that the harvest this year (where there is no fighting) will be very small. In the actual zone of operations there will probably be none at all.

Reports are coming from a dozen different quarters of the condition of the Germans. A story from a source which in many months I have found always trustworthy indicates that the soldiers are surrendering to the Russians in small batches whenever a favourable opportunity offers.

The reported complaint is that their rations are increasingly short and that there is growing discouragement. There are dozens of similar stories circulated every day. One does not perhaps accept them at par, but the great significance is that they are circulating here now for practically the first time. When I was last in Warsaw I questioned many prisoners but never found one who would criticize his own fare. This condition seems to have changed materially in the past ten weeks. No one however must dream of underestimating the stamina of the enemy on this Front; for however one's sympathy may go, they are a brave and stubborn foe, and months may elapse, even after they begin to weaken in *moral*, before the task of beating them will be an easy one. Their lines on this Front are reported to be extremely strong, and I am told by an observer that they are employing a new type of barbed wire which is extremely difficult to cut, and presents increased difficulty in breaking through.

The condition of the Russians is infinitely better than at any time since the war started. Their 1915 levies, which are just coming into the field now in great blocks, are about the finest raw fighting material that one can find in Europe. Great, strapping, healthy, good-natured lads who look as though they never had a day's sickness in their life. I think I do not exaggerate when I say that I have seen nearly 100,000 of these new levies and I have yet to see a battalion that did not exhale high spirits and enthusiasm. They come swinging through Warsaw, laughing and singing with a confidence and optimism which it is hard to believe possible when one considers that we are in the 9th month of the war. Surely if the Germans, who are straining every effort now to raise new troops, could see these men that Russia is pouring into the field they would have a genuine qualm as to the future. And these are but a drop in the bucket to what is available in great Russia that lies behind. Over here there will never be any lack of men, and the Czar can keep putting troops just like this into the field for as many more years as the war may last. After nearly a year on this Front of the war, one just begins to appreciate the enormous human resources which Russia has at her command in this great conflict.

During the winter there was a pretty widespread apprehension of conditions which might result among the soldiers when the spring and warm weather came. As far as one can learn, the authorities have made a great effort to improve sanitary conditions at the Front, and there is very little sickness in the army at present. Those who are in a position to know, seem to feel confident that such steps as are necessary to maintain the health of the men at a high standard during the summer have been taken. It is certain that there has been a pretty general clean up, and that there is less disease now, even with the warmer weather, than there was in February.

In the meantime, the Spring has come and the roads are rapidly drying up. The occasional rumours of the Germans reaching Warsaw are becoming more and more rare, and the gossip of the town now is as to what date will be selected for the Russian advance.

Russian bath train.

The life of the city is absolutely normal, and I am told that the shopkeepers are doing a bigger business than ever before. The restaurants are preparing for their out-of-door cafés, and the streets are bright with the uniforms of the Russian soldiery. A German officer who came through here the other day (as a prisoner) could not believe his eyes. "Why," he is reported to have said to his Russian captor, "we supposed Warsaw was abandoned by everyone who could get away. But the town seems as usual." And the officer was right. The casual observer finds it hard to realize that there is a line of battle only 30 miles away.

CHAPTER III
AN AMERICAN DOCTOR IN THE RUSSIAN ARMY

Dated:
WARSAW, POLAND,
May 3, 1915.

IT is a far cry from the city of Seattle in the State of Washington, U.S.A., to the little village of Sejny in the Polish government of Suwalki, but this is the jump that one must make to follow the career of Dr. Eugene Hurd, the only American surgeon attached to the Russian Red Cross working in the field in this war. Inasmuch as the story of the Doctor is a good one in itself, and as from him one learns not a little about the Field Hospital service of the Russians, it seems quite worth while to devote a chapter to this very interesting and useful individual.

Up to August last Dr. Hurd was a practising surgeon in Seattle, a member of the State Legislature and spoken of as coming Mayor of the town. When he strolled casually into my room at Warsaw in the uniform of a Russian Colonel, who spoke not a word of any language except English, I was naturally somewhat surprised. "How on earth," I asked him, "do you happen to be in the Russian Army?" Unbuckling his sword and sprawling his six feet three of brawn and sinew in an armchair he began his story.

"Well, it was this way. I've never had much time to follow politics in Europe, as my time's been pretty much occupied cutting off legs and arms and such, out on the Pacific Coast. But my people have always been regular Americans, and some of us have been in every war the U.S.A. ever pulled off. My great-grandfather fought in the revolution; my grandfather in the Mexican war, and my father in the Civil and Spanish-American wars. Well, I was raised in an army post, and ever since I was a kid I've heard my father talk about how Russia stuck with us during the Civil war. When things looked blue and bad for the North she sent her old fleet over, and let it set right there in New York Harbour until required, if needed. During the war in Manchuria we were all for Russia on just this account, and when she got licked Dad and I both felt bad. All right. Well one day out in Seattle I read in the paper that Germany had declared war on Russia. I remembered that business, back in the '60's,' and what the Russians did for us, and I just said to myself, 'Well, I'm for Russia anyhow,' and I sat down that very day and wrote to the head of the medical department at Petrograd, and just told them straight that we had always been for Russia ever since that business of her fleet, and that if I could serve her in this war I'd come over even if I had to throw up my own practice, which by the way is a pretty good one.

"Well, a couple of months went by and I had forgotten all about it when one day the Russian Consul blew into my office with a cable from Petrograd, a bunch of money in one hand and a ticket over the Siberian in the other. So I just locked up my office and came right over. In Petrograd they ran me around in an auto. for two days, and then shipped me down to Grodno, where I got a Colonel's uniform and went right out to the 'Front' in charge of a Field Hospital, where I've been now for three solid months, and you're the first American I've seen and you certainly look good to me," and the Doctor smiled genially.

I have got more information about the Russian wounded from Hurd than any man I have met since I came to Russia, and though he does not speak the language he sees everything. He was at once placed in charge of an outfit of sixty-one men and five wagons which formed a Field Hospital. "I have my bunch well organized," the doctor said. "You see I handled it this way. I divided all my outfit, medicine chest, instruments, etc., so that they went into the five wagons. Each wagon was painted a certain colour and every box that went into that wagon had a band of the same colour around it and a number. I had a man for each box and each knew exactly what to do. I can halt on the march and my men are so well trained now that I can commence operating in ten minutes after we make a stop. I can quit work and be packed up and on the march again in twenty. I like these fellows over here fine, and when I once get them properly broken in, they work splendidly." [The Field Hospital to which he was attached was up in the rear of the Russian lines all during the recent fighting in East Prussia.] "I never worked so hard in my life," he continued. "One day I had 375 men come to my table between sunset and morning and I was working steadily until the next night, making twenty-three hours without intermission. It was a tough job because every little while we had to pull up stakes and move off to the rear with our wounded. That made it hard for us and difficult to do real good work."

The Emperor with his Staff.

Russian nurses attend to the feeding of the soldiers.

The work and experience with the Russian wounded have given this American doctor a remarkable insight into the character of the peasant soldier. "These moujik chaps," he assured me, "never make a complaint. I never saw anything like it. Sometimes they groan a little when you're digging for a bullet, but once off the table and in the straw (we are without beds as we move too fast for that) a whole barnful will be as quiet as though the place was empty; one German, on the other hand, will holler his head off and keep the whole place awake. The Russians never complain, and everything you do for them they appreciate remarkably. I do a lot of doctoring for the villagers, and every day there's a line a block long waiting to get some 'American' dope, and they're so grateful it makes you feel ashamed. Everybody wants to kiss your hands. I tried putting my hands behind me, but those that were behind were just as bad as those in front. Now I've given up and just let them kiss."

The vitality of the Russian soldier is amazing according to the evidence of this observer. With the exception of wounds in the heart, spine or big arteries there is nothing that must certainly prove fatal. Many head wounds that seem incredibly dangerous recover. "I had one case," he told me, "which I never would have believed. The soldier walked into my hospital with a bullet through his head. It had come out just above his left ear and I had to dissect away part of the brain that was lying on the ear, Well, that fellow talked all through the dressing and walked out of the hospital. I sent him to the rear and I have no doubt that he recovered absolutely."

In the hundreds of cases operated on not a single death occurred on the operating table and not one lung wound proved fatal. Many of the abdominal wounds of the worst type make ultimate recoveries, and it was the opinion of the surgeon that not above five to ten per cent. of the patients who reached the first dressing stations died later from the effects of their wounds. That the war was very popular among the common soldiers was the conclusion that my friend had reached. "The old men with families don't care much for it," he added, "but that is because they are always worrying about their families at home, but the young fellows are keen for it, anxious to get to the 'Front' when they first come out, and eager to get back to it even after they have been wounded. Some of them as a matter of fact go back several times after being in the hospital."

In discussing the comparative merits of the Germans and Russians, it was his opinion that though the Germans were better rifle shots, they could not compare with the Russians when it came to the bayonet. "When these moujiks," said the doctor, "climb out of their trenches and begin to sing their national songs, they just go crazy and they aren't scared of anything; and believe me, when the Germans see them coming across the fields bellowing these songs of theirs, they just don't wait one minute, but dig right out across the landscape as fast as they can tear. I don't think there's a soldier in the world that has anything on the Russian private for bravery. They are a stubborn lot too, and will sit in trenches in all weathers and be just as cheerful under one condition as another. One big advantage over here, as I regard it, is the good relations between the soldiers and the officers."

One extremely significant statement as to the German losses in the East Prussian movement was made by this American surgeon. The church and convent where his hospital is located were previously used for the same purposes by the Germans. According to the statement of the priest who was there during their occupation, 10,500 German wounded were handled in that one village in a period of six weeks and one day. From this number of wounded in one village may be estimated what the loss to the enemy must have been during the entire campaign on the East Prussian Front.

CHAPTER IV
GENERAL RUSSKY'S SUCCESSOR

Dated:

WARSAW, RUSSIA,
May 10, 1915.

THE two most simple personalities that I have met in this war are the Grand Duke Nicholas, and the Commander who has come to the Northern Armies to take up the post made vacant by the retirement of General Russky. Certain business relating to desired freedom of movement in the zone of operations took the writer to the head-quarters of General Alexieff, which is situated in a place not very far away. Without giving away any figures it is perhaps safe to say that the command of General Alexieff is twice the size of that now under Field-Marshal Sir John French on the continent. The territory occupied by the armies commanded by him covers an enormous area, and probably up to this war there has been no single individual in the history of the world with such a vast military organization as that over which General Alexieff presides as supreme dictator, subject only to the Grand Duke himself. The whole aspect of the headquarters of which he is the presiding genius is, in atmosphere, the last word in the modern idea of a commanding general's place of abode. The town in which he is living is perhaps a model one from the point of view of the gentlemen who write the textbooks and sketch the details of the programme and course which should be adopted by military chiefs. The theory in the Japanese Army was that the brains of the army should be so far away from the actual scene of operations, that the officer would be absolutely detached from the atmosphere of war; and that between himself and the Front there should be installed so many nervous shock absorbers that the office of the great chief himself should be the realm of pure reason with no noise nor excitement nor hurrying aides to impair his judgment.

I recall a conversation I once had with Major (now Lt.-General) Tanaka, Oyama's personal A.D.C. "I should have liked to have been with the General Staff," I remarked to him, "during the Battle of Moukden. It must have been an exciting time with you." My friend laughed and answered, "You would have had a great surprise, I imagine. There was no excitement at all. How do you suppose Oyama and his staff spent much of their time during the battle?" One naturally imagined that it was spent scrutinizing maps and making plans, and I said this to Tanaka. "Not at all," he replied, "when the battle began, our work was largely finished. It was but necessary to make an occasional change in the line here and there, and this too, for only a few minutes of the time of the Field-Marshal. Most of the time he and Kodame (Chief of General Staff) were playing croquet."

Much the same atmosphere of detachment from the activities of the campaign may be seen to-day in the little Polish city where Alexieff has his head-quarters, except that no one here has time for croquet. It is a safe venture that outside of his own staff there are not fifty soldiers in the whole town. It is in fact less military in appearance than any city I have ever seen since I have have been in Russia. In front of his office are a couple of soldiers, and a small Russian flag hangs over the door. Nothing outside would lead one to believe that within is the man in the palm of whose hand lies the fate and movements of hundreds upon hundreds of thousands of men, and at whose word a thousand guns will spread death and destruction. In trenches miles away, stretching through forest and along hilltops, numberless regiments and brigades await the curt order from this building to launch themselves against the German lines.

The man himself is as quiet and unobtrusive as are his surroundings. Perhaps fifty-eight or fifty-nine in years with a very intellectual face and an almost shy manner, is Alexieff, the man whom current gossip credits with the keenest brain in the Russian field armies. As Ivanov's Chief of Staff, he is said to have been a great factor in the planning and the execution of much of the Galician campaign, and those who know him well, believe that under his direction great things will be accomplished in Poland. The General is very quiet and retiring, and from a very brief observation one would say that he was primarily a man of strategy, more at home solving the intellectual problems of a campaign than in working out tactical puzzles in the field.

The staff of the quiet unostentatious Russian who is commanding this enormous front consists of about seventy-five members (about the same number as Kusmanek of Przemysl fame had on his personal staff for the defence of the city), and taken as a whole, they are most serious and hard-working men, if their looks do not belie them. "You would be surprised," an A.D.C. informed me, "to know the enormous amount of work that we all get through here. There is a lull on this front now, and it is comparatively an easy time, but in spite of that fact we are all of us busy from morning until night. When there is a movement under way we do not get any rest even at nights." One comes from Warsaw where rumours are flying thick and fast as to German advances and Russian mishaps, to find everything serene and calm and the general opinion of the staff one of great optimism. For the moment the Russians are in the trough of the sea, as it were, and all of the late news from Galicia is not particularly favourable; but if the attitude of the staff is any criterion, the situation is not felt to be of a critical nature, and for the first time in months one hears officers expressing the opinion that the war will end this year.

There is a tendency to welcome the German impetuosity of attack, for each fresh irruption means a weakening of the enemy. The Russian theory is that

Russia can stand the losses, large as they are, almost indefinitely, and that she is willing to take the burden of breaking the German wave again and again if need be, knowing that each assault of the enemy is bringing them nearer and nearer to the end of their tether. Since the latest irruption into Galicia we hear less talk of a Russian advance in the near future, but certainly not a sign of discouragement in any of the high quarters. One may well believe that this last outburst was not anticipated, but the Russians over on this side are as ready to "play" the fish now as they were when the war first started. It was hoped after the January-February attacks, that the enemy was exhausted and the time was in sight when the gaff might be of use. Now the fish has taken another spurt, and the Russians are letting out the line again and are prepared to let it have another fling in their waters. But they believe none the less that the enemy is firmly hooked, and that it is merely a question of time when from sheer exhaustion he will tire and they may begin to drive home their own attacks.

The Russian attitude is very philosophical, and though a people who are temperamentally not without a vein of melancholy, they take this war with much more equanimity than one could have imagined possible. Retreats and shifting of lines no longer create panics over here. People are sorry. They had hoped that the Germans were nearer the point of exhaustion, but there is not the slightest indication of discouragement. Probably their attitude is due primarily to the fact that they had never anticipated an easy victory nor a short war. They knew from the start that they were in for a terrific ordeal, and what goes on day after day, with its ebbs and its floods, is merely a matter of the day's work with them. They have seen again and again the irruptions of the Germans gradually absorbed by their troops, and each set back now is accepted as only temporary. The movement of the Germans in Courland has hardly made any impression at all in Russia generally, if the reports one hears are true.

Russian soldiers performing their native dance.

The Russians had practically no troops in that province, which itself offered no great strategic advantage to the Germans. Taking advantage of this weak spot, the Germans with a number of corps—it is placed as high as three—poured into the almost unprotected country.

The Russians say that the German motive is first that they would be able to announce to their people that they had occupied enemy territory, and second that the rich province would give them certain much needed supplies. For a day or two the progress seems to have been almost without interruption, but now we hear that it has been checked and that the enemy are gradually giving way before the Russians, who have shifted troops to that front to prevent further advances. The occupation of Libau does not seem to worry any one very much. "What good will it do them?" one Russian officer said to me? "No doubt they will fortify it and make it as strong as possible. Probably we will never try to get it back while the war lasts. Why should we? It is of no great value strategically, and it is not worth the price of lives and troops detached from other points to retake it. When we have won, it will naturally come back to us without our having to spend a single extra life in getting it."

The situation in Galicia is still something of a puzzle, but those in authority do not seem to be taking it over seriously. There is reason to believe that it is a repetition of what has occurred again and again on this and other fronts. The Germans, by means of their superior rail facilities made a sudden concentration and hit the Russian line with such energy as to force its retirement. Each mile of the Russian retreat has strengthened their army by the additions of reserves, while it has probably seen an increasing weakening of the enemies'. The sudden advance of the enemy has forced the withdrawal of the Russians pushing through the Dukla, who were obviously menaced in their communications. I am told now that the German attacks have already passed their zenith, and that the Russians reinforced by new troops are confident of checking any further advance. Over here it is but a question of breaking the first fury of the attack. When that is done we can count on the Russian muoujik slowly but surely to force his way back over the lost ground. The end of the incident sees the Russians stronger and the Germans weaker. It is futile for any one to attempt to estimate how many more of these irruptions the Germans are capable of, but we are certain that be it this summer or next there is a limit to them. When that limit has been reached the Russian advance will begin.

CHAPTER V
CHECKING UP THE SITUATION IN POLAND

Dated:
WARSAW,
May 24, 1915.

A FEW weeks ago the writer expressed the opinion that a permanent optimism had come to Warsaw. For several weeks this impression seemed to have every justification in fact, but since the commencement of the Galician movement in the south the confidence felt by the saner members of the community has been utterly submerged by the pessimism which in waves has swept over the town. One finds it impossible to know definitely from what exact quarters all the false stories start, and if one tries to run them down the *trail* speedily vanishes. The explanation is that the Jews in Poland are so unfriendly to Russian interests and Russian successes, that the slightest set-back, or rumour of bad news, is seized on by them, and in a few hours is spread all over the town, exaggerated grossly with every telling. It is really extraordinary, after ten months of war, how persistent these hostile factions are in their hope of German success. There are, besides the Jews, probably many Austrian agents, who use the slightest pretext to start stories in the hope of creating a panic.

Within the last two weeks every imaginable tale has been current. Last week there was so much vagueness in regard to the news coming up from the south of Poland, that it seemed wise to make a quick tour in the rear of the Russian positions in order to get some opinion of the real situation. The collection of war news falls very definitely into two classes, descriptive writing and material which is merely indicative of the situation as a whole. The former is of course more interesting to the average reader, but the latter is far more important from every other angle. After ten months of war, the vital question now is whether the Germans are advancing or retiring, and not so much how the battles themselves are conducted, or what sort of a picture is presented in the different actions. So my trip of yesterday, though not in the least picturesque in its happenings, was extremely interesting in that it offered an emphatic contradiction to practically every adverse rumour that had gained currency in Warsaw for the week previously.

The Polish Legion. Note the small boy in the ranks as mascot.

We left Warsaw at six in the morning in our racing car, and as soon as we were clear of the town and headed in the direction of Radom, on the fine macadam highway, we were able to develop a speed that no express train in Russia has made since the declaration of war. This highway has been the artery of travel and communication over which ammunition, transport and guns have moved almost without interruption for ten months. That the Russians have kept it in good condition, is apparent from the fact that we were able to make above 65 versts an hour on many stretches of the way. I passed over the same road many times during the first months of the war, and its condition now is infinitely better than it was in those days.

On every hand are evidences of increased Russian efficiency. The war now has become strictly a matter of organization, and everything goes on now without excitement and without confusion of any sort. Road gangs have been organized, and these highways are maintained with as much care as the permanent way of a railway line. One sign of the times is the new departure of the Russian authorities, in building at intervals of about every 5 versts a boiled water station, which is distinguished by a special flag. Here in a shed closed on three sides is a great boiler with numerous taps on it. When troops are passing in any quantities the water is kept hot that the soldiers may always get boiling water for their tea. When there is small movement on the road, they can always get it cold for drinking purposes.

As it was Sunday we found the road practically free of transport. Barring occasional soldiers sauntering along the highway there was no sign of war until we were within a few miles of Radom, when, perhaps 20 versts to the west, columns of smoke, drifting lazily off in the still air, indicated where some German battery had been shelling some unfortunate village. Away off on the horizon a few faint puffs of white in the blue showed where our batteries were breaking shrapnel under a speck of an aeroplane, which had evidently been on a morning tour of inspection. I was rather curious to see Radom, because for a week we had been told in Warsaw that a terrible panic prevailed here, and that the population were leaving in a frenzy of terror to avoid the sweep of the Germans on Warsaw, that same old story which has for so many months been circulated by the Jewish population. But Radom itself was as quiet and casual as a city of the same size in far off America might have been on a Sunday morning. The streets were crowded with the population in their best clothes going to church, and the panic so widely discussed in Warsaw was conspicuous by its absence.

I talked with a number of the townspeople, and they were as surprised as they could be to know that they were all (according to Warsaw) in full flight for the other side of the Vistula. What astonishes one most is the absolute lack of information in one place of what is going on in the next town. Kielce is but 30 miles from Radom, yet I could find no one, neither officer nor civilian, who could say positively whether on this particular day it was in our hands or in the hands of the enemy. We did learn however from an officer that the road had been badly cut up, and that fighting had taken place near Kielce, with destruction of bridges, which would make it impossible for us to get there in a car. As a fact, I learned later in the day that the road for perhaps 15 versts north of Kielce was held by German cavalry, and so was just as well satisfied that we had not gone that way.

Radom I found was outside the army group which I had a special permit to visit, and it was therefore necessary to call on the General commanding the army before I could with propriety pay a visit to any of the corps commanders in this theatre of war. It was necessary, therefore, to motor to a certain point east of the Vistula to pay our respects to this gentleman. Well on in the afternoon we motored into the beautiful grounds of a Polish villa and spent several hours with one of the men who, with a number of corps, was able to contribute an important part to the defeat of the Austrians on the Grodek line in the fall of last year. Here we were cordially received both by the General and by his staff, two of whom at once ordered refreshments for us and remained with us until we started back for Warsaw late in the day.

From this point we were in touch with the sources of information flowing in from both Southern Poland and the great battlefield in Galicia. All the Russian corps in Poland, with the exception of one that lay next the Vistula, had been inactive during the past weeks, and after shifting their position to the new line, made necessary by the retirement of the Galician army, had been ordered to remain strictly on the defensive. The corps lying next the

Vistula, however, was only across the river from the great action going on south of them, and after days of listening to the roar of their brothers' cannon to the south, they were in anything but a placid or quiet mood. The whole line, in fact, was figuratively being held on the leash, but this last corps had been so infected by the contagion of the action to the south that it proved very difficult to keep the units in their trenches. At the first feeler of the German advance, which came up on their side of the Vistula, they at once jumped at the conclusion that the best defensive was a strong attack, and with this idea in mind they considered, no doubt, that they were strictly in accord with their defensive orders when they attacked the Germans.

The Vistula (winter).

Soldiers are seen in the picture destroying the broken ice. This is a great danger to the bridges when carried away by the current.

The ball was started, as far as I can learn, by a cavalry colonel who, with a small command, attacked a pontoon bridge train that, in some incredible way, was poking along in advance with only a meagre escort. The advance of this small unit of horsemen served as a spark in the Russian powder magazine, and within a few hours the whole corps was engaged in an attack on the German infantry. It is hard to get any accurate details of the operations, but this fighting lasted probably two to three days. The ardent Russian regiments fell on the centre of a German formation, which was said to be the 46th Landsturm corps, smashed its centre and dissipated its flanking supports of a division each. The Russians claim that 12,000 were left on the field and that they took 6,000 prisoners. In any case there is no question that this action put out at least one corps from further activity as an efficient unit.

The German prisoners captured expressed themselves as greatly surprised at the Russians attacking them. They had been told that the Russians had all crossed the Vistula and were in rapid retreat to the west, and that the probabilities were that the road to Moscow would be open in a few weeks. From various members of the Russian Staff I obtained many details as to the fighting in Galicia, which all agreed had been terrific but was going extremely well for them on the line of the San river. It is too soon to attempt a detailed account of this action, but it will form one of the greatest stories of the whole war when the returns are all in. Suffice it to say that the Russians had been aware of the impending attack for several weeks, and had been preparing, in case of necessity, a retirement on to a position upon the San river with Przemysl as the salient thereof.

This Russian retreat did not come as a surprise even to the writer. As far back as a month ago he was aware of feverish activities in rehabilitating the Przemysl defences, and though at that time the object was vague, it became clear enough when this crisis broke that the Russians had foreseen the possibility of the failure to hold the Dunajec line. The Germans carried this by a concentration of artillery fire, probably greater even than that of the English guns at Neuve Chapelle. So fierce was this torrent of flying steel that the Russian line was eaten away in the centre, and in the Carpathian flank, and there seems reason to believe that the army on the Dunajec was cut in three sections when it began to retire. That it pulled itself together and has been able to hold itself intact on the San up to the time of this writing is evidence of the resiliency of the Russian organization.

The Russians having had the alternative in view, withdrew with great speed, destroying bridges and approaches in order to delay the Germans. In the meantime both their reserves of men and munitions were being pushed up to await them on the San line. When the Germans came up in strength with their tongues hanging out, and their formations suffering from lack of rest and lack of ammunition, they found the Russian line waiting for them. It is futile to estimate the German losses at this time, but they will be in the hundreds of thousands, and a final count will show them to be at least two to three times greater than the Russian sacrifices. A German prisoner is said to have made the complaint that the Russians fought like barbarians. "Had they been civilized people," he is reported to have said, "they would have stayed on the Dunajec and fought like men. In that case we would have utterly destroyed their army." Instead of that they went away and fought on the San. What seems to have happened is that the Germans were not actually short of ammunition, but in extending their line to the San they could not bring it up with the same rapidity as in the Dunajec and Carpathian attacks;

the result was that they were unable to feed their guns according to their new artillery programme begun on the Dunajec line, a programme no doubt borrowed from the west.

CHAPTER VI
A VISIT TO THE POSITIONS

From:
SOMEWHERE ON THE RAWKA LINE,
May 25, 1915.

DURING the comparative lull on the Bzura-Rawka-Pilitza line I have been trying to go about to certain important salients on our front and have a look both at the terrain, and the positions which we are defending.

Leaving Warsaw by motor we ran out to the head-quarters of a certain army where we found the General living in the palace of a Polish noble. Beautiful avenues of trees gave access to a wonderful garden with a little lake before an old mansion dating back to the eighteenth century. Here in the quiet seclusion of a little forest lives the general, who presides over the destinies of perhaps 150,000 men. We are received cordially by the Chief of Staff who, with exemplary patience, reads over the twelve permits of various sorts which complete the constantly growing collection of authorizations for me to come and go on this front. After careful scrutiny of all he sighs heavily, for perhaps he is not an admirer of the press, but none the less he inquires cordially what we would like to do. "Heavy batteries and observation points" is always my reply for reasons already explained. A smart young aide is sent for who, it appears, speaks English fluently, having lived for some time in America. The staff offer us an additional automobile, and while this is being brought round we sit out under the trees in the garden. Just behind the house, in a bower, is another officer of the staff sitting in an easy-chair behind a table before which stand a group of Austrian prisoners whom he is examining for information. After a few minutes our young aide comes back, and with two automobiles we start for the positions.

We must first go to the head-quarters of an army corps. This is distant 25 versts, and as the roads are for the most part short cuts across the fields, it takes us more than an hour to reach a very unpretentious village where we meet the General commanding the — Corps. This man is distinctly of the type that war produces. He was only a minor general when the war started, but efficiency in action has given him two promotions. Shabby and war-worn he is living in a mere hovel, still wearing the uniform and shoulder straps of two grades back when he was a somewhat humble officer in the artillery. By him we are supplied with a soldier guide and go off to the head-quarters of an artillery brigade where we find the commander of the guns who provides us with a member of his staff. This officer joins our party, and directs us to the head-quarters of an artillery unit composed of a number of batteries. I say unit because it is all controlled from one point of observation.

By the time we pull up between a couple of ruined peasants' homes, only the walls of which are standing; it is after seven in the evening. From a kind of cave among the debris there emerged three or four tired-looking artillerymen who are in charge of the guns in these positions. The country here is flat and rolling, with a little ridge to the west of us, which cuts off the view into the valley beyond, in which are the lines of the Russian and German trenches. Leaving our automobiles in the road, we stroll through a wheat-field toward the ridge, distant perhaps 1,000 yards. In the corner of the field is a hedge, and behind the hedge is a battery of field guns. One notices with each passing month the increasing cleverness of the Russians in masking their batteries. Though this is no wood, we walk almost on to the position before we discover the guns at all. They are well dug in, with small fir trees borrowed from neighbouring bits of woodland stuck in the ground all about them. Each gun is separated from its brother by a screen of green, and boughs above mask the view from an aeroplane. From the front one would never see them at all unless one were looking closely. To-night the last red rays from the setting sun just catch a twinkle of the steel in their shining throats, as their long sleek snouts protrude from the foliage. The shields are painted a kind of green which helps still more to make them invisible.

This particular battery, so its Colonel tells us, has had a great laugh on the enemy during the past few days. What happened was this. A German Taube flew over the line several times, and it kept coming back so frequently and hovering over the battery, that the officers who were watching it became suspicious that they had been spotted. When darkness fell the entire personnel of the battery became extremely busy, and by working like bees they moved their guns perhaps 600 yards to the south and by daylight had them in the new positions and fairly well masked. Shortly after sunrise back came the aeroplane, and when over the old position it gave a signal to its own lines and then flew back. Almost instantly hell broke loose on the abandoned spot. In walking over the ground one is amazed at the accuracy of long range artillery fire, for in the ten-acre lot in which the old position was the centre there was hardly ten square yards without its shell hole, while the ground was a junk heap of steel and shrapnel fragments. Six hundred yards away the men of the battery watched it all and laughed their sides out at the way they had fooled the Germans. This particular battery had bothered the enemy a great deal and they were on the look out for it. Probably there will be further competitions of wits before the week is out. From glancing at the field torn up with shell fire one begins to realize what observation means to the enemy. With modern methods a single signal from an aeroplane may mean the wiping out in a few minutes of an unsuspecting battery that has been safely hidden for months.

Leaving the guns, we saunter across the wheat-field toward the ridge, the great red ball of the setting sun dazzling our eyes with its aspect of molten steel. On the very crest of the rolling ground is a grove of stunted firs, and through this lies a path to the observation trench which is entered by an approach growing gradually deeper until, cutting through the very ridge, it ends in the observation trench dug out of the earth on the western slope. For the last couple of hundred yards before we enter the approaches, we are in plain view of the German gunners, but we had supposed that at the distance a few men would not be noticed. Evidently, however, our observers in the German line have had their eyes glued on this spot, for we had barely entered the trench when a shell burst down in front of us. The writer was looking through the hyperscope at the time, but imagined that it was at least half a mile away. An instant later came the melancholy wail of another shell over our heads and the report of its explosion half way between us and our motor-car in the road. Behind it came another and another each one getting nearer our trench. The last one passed a few feet over our heads and burst just beyond, covering us in the trench with dust and filling our nostrils with the fumes of gunpowder. Another shortening up of the range might have landed in our delightful retreat, but evidently the Germans became discouraged, for we heard nothing more from them.

Through the hyperscopes one could look out over the beautiful sweep of the valley studded with little farms, the homes of which are mostly in ruins. This point from which we were studying the landscape was only 100 yards from our own line of trenches, which lay just in front of and below us, while not more than 75 yards beyond were the line of the German trenches. So clear were they in the field of the hyperscope that one could actually see the loopholes in the ridge of earth. Our own were, of course, open from the back, and one could see the soldiers moving about in their quarters or squatting comfortably against the walls of the trenches. Away to the west were ridges of earth here and there, where our friends of the artillery told us were reserve trenches, while they pointed out groves of trees or ruined villages in which they suspected lurked the German guns.

Russian officers in an artillery observation position.

After the report of the shells had died away and the dust settled there was the silence of absolute peace and serenity over the whole valley. Not a rifle shot or a human noise broke the beautiful calm of the May sunset. Off to the west glimmered the silver stream of the Rawka. To look out over this lovely valley in the falling twilight it seemed incredible that thousands of men lay concealed under our very eyes, men who were waiting only a favourable opportunity to leap out of their trenches and meet each other in hand-to-hand combat. On the advice of our guides, we waited in our secure little trench until the last red rays of the sun were cut off by the horizon in the west, when we returned by the way we had come to the waiting automobiles.

The whole valley in this section is very flat, and the ridges such as the one I have described are very scarce. The Russian lines are extremely strong, and one gets the idea that they would require a good deal of taking before the Germans could occupy them. Our artillery seemed to be in excellent quantities, and the ammunition situation satisfactory if the officer may be believed. The rears of all these positions have been prepared for defence, and there are at least three lines or groups of trenches lying between this front and Warsaw, each of which would present as strong a defence as the line which now for many months has defied all efforts of the enemy to get through.

I was especially interested in looking over this locality, because in Warsaw it has been mentioned as a point where the Russians were in great danger, and where they were barely able to hold their own. The truth is that there has been little fighting here for months excepting an occasional burst of artillery, or now and then a spasm of inter-trench fighting between unimportant units. I told our guide of the dismal stories we heard, and he only laughed as he pointed out to me a level stretch of country on our side of the ridge. A number of young Russian officers were riding about on prancing horses. "See there," my friend told me, "we have laid out a race course, and the day after to-morrow the officers of this brigade are going to have a steeplechase. You see they have built a little platform for the general to stand on and judge the events. We are only 1,000 yards here from the trenches of the enemy. So you see we do not feel as anxious about the safety of our position as they do in Warsaw." He lighted a cigarette and then added seriously: "No, the Germans cannot force us here, nor do I think on any of the other Warsaw fronts. Our positions have never been as strong as they are to-day."

A few minutes later we were in our motors speeding through the twilight to the village in our rear where the Chief of Staff of the — Corps had arranged quarters for us.

CHAPTER VII
A SUMMER DAY ON THE RAWKA LINE

From:

A CERTAIN ARMY CORPS HEAD-QUARTERS NOT FAR FROM
THE RAWKA.
May 26, 1915.

THE month of May in Poland, if this season is typical of the climate here, is a period to dream about. When we turned out of our camp beds early this morning, the sun was streaming into our little whitewashed room, while the fragrance of lilacs blooming in a near-by garden drifted in at the open window. In the little garden behind our house are a dozen colonies of bees, and already they are up and about their daily tasks. The sky is without a cloud and the warmth and life of the early spring morning makes one forget the terrible business that we are engaged in. The little street of the town is lined with great horse-chestnut trees now in full bloom with every branch laden deep with the great white pendent blossoms. For a moment one stands drinking in the beauty of the new day and the loveliness of the morning, with one's mind drifting far, far away to other scenes where flowers too are blooming at this season of the year. But as our eyes wander down the street, the thoughts of gentler things are suddenly dissipated, and with a jolt one's mind comes back to the work-a-day world whose daily task now is the destruction of an enemy in the line of trenches not so many miles away.

What has broken the peaceful tremor of our thoughts is the sight of some soldiers pulling into the town a half-wrecked aeroplane brought down by artillery fire the day before near our lines. Its wings are shattered and its propellers twisted into kindling, while its slight body (if one can use that expression) is torn and punctured by a score or more of shrapnel holes, with several gashes where bits of the shell case had penetrated the thin metal frame. Here at least is one example of artillery practice which has been able to cripple the bird of ill omen on the wing. After a generous breakfast, provided by our kind host the General, we are in our motor-cars again and in a few minutes are speeding down one of the roads westward to the head-quarters of a certain artillery brigade who over the telephone have consented to show us particular choice sights that they have on exhibition on their front.

Every village that we pass through is full of soldiers bestirring for the day, while already the main arteries of travel to the trenches are filling up with the activities of the morning. It is a perfectly still day, and with each advancing hour it is growing hotter. There has been no rain for a week or two, the dust is deep upon the roads, and as our cars hum along the highways we leave volumes of the thin cloud in our wake. Now and again we pass small columns of infantry marching cheerfully along in the sunshine, each man in a cloud of dust. Yet every face is cheerful, and almost without exception the men are singing their marching songs as they swing along the highways. In the villages and on the road everything suggests war, but now with quite a different atmosphere from that of last autumn. Then it was war also, but of war the novelty, the new and the untried. Then all faces were anxious, some apprehensive, some depressed. They were going into a new experience. Now, however, it is war as a tried and experienced profession that is about us.

The conduct of the campaign has become as much of a business to the soldiers and to the officers as the operating of a railroad to men engaged in running it. The deaths and the wounds have become to these men we see now simply a part of their profession, and they have seen so much of this side of the business that it has long since been discounted. The whole atmosphere of the front as we see it in May is as that of a permanent state of society. These men look as though they had been fighting for ten years and expected to be fighting for the rest of their days. War has become the commonplace and peace seems the unreality.

At brigade head-quarters we halt a few minutes and are directed to proceed slowly along a certain road, and advised to stop in a cut just before passing over a certain crest. When we learn that the enemy's guns command the road over the crest we inquire with the keenest interest the exact location of the ridge mentioned, for something suggests to us that this is a bit of interesting information that the artillery officer is handing out to us so very casually. They are all casual by the way; probably they have all got so used to sudden death and destruction that they feel as nonchalant about their own fate as they do about others. Half an hour's run over very heavy and sandy road, brought us on to a great white ribbon of a highway that ran due west and dipped over the ridge.

This was our place, and stopping the cars we climbed out to meet a few officers sauntering down the road. They seemed to be coming from nowhere in particular, but as I learned later, they lived in a kind of cave dug out of the side of the road, and had been advised by telephone that we were coming and so were on the lookout for us. The ranking officer was a colonel of artillery—one of the kind that you would turn about in the street to look at and to say to yourself, "Every inch a soldier." A serious, kindly-faced man in a dirty uniform with shoulder straps so faded and frayed that a second look was necessary to get his rank at all. For six months he had been living in just such quarters as the cave in the side of the road where we found him. He was glad to show us his observation. One could see at a glance that his whole heart and soul were wrapped up in his three batteries, and he spoke of all his positions and his observation points with as much pride as a mother speaking about her children.

The country here is a great sweeping expanse, with just a few ridges here and there like the one that we have come up behind. The country reminds one of the valley of the Danube or perhaps the Red River Valley in North Dakota, except that the latter has less timber in it. We are ourselves quite uncertain as to where the enemy's position is, for in the sweep of the valley there is little to indicate the presence of any army at all, or to suggest the possibility of hostilities from any quarter. I asked one of the officers who strolled along with us where the German lines were. "Oh, over there," he remarked, casually waving his hand in a northerly direction. "Probably they can see us then," I suggested. Personally I felt a mild curiosity in the subject which apparently my companion did not share. He stopped and offered me a cigarette, and as he lighted one himself, he murmured indifferently, "Yes, I dare say they could see us if they turned their glasses on this ridge. But probably they won't. Can I give you a light?"

I thanked him politely and also commended the sun for shining in the enemy's eyes instead of over their shoulders as happened last night when the observer in the German battery spotted us at 6,000 yards and sent five shells to tell us that we were receiving his highest consideration. On the top of a near-by hill was a small building which had formerly been the Russian observation point, but the Germans suspecting this had quickly reduced it to a pile of ruins. Near by we entered a trench cut in from the back of the hill, and worked our way up to an observation station cut out of the side of the slope in front of the former position.

A first-line trench in Poland.

It was now getting on toward noon and intensely hot. The view from this position as one could sweep it with the hyperscope was perfectly beautiful. Off to the west twinkled the silver ribbon of the Rawka, while the whole plain was dotted with fields of wheat and rye that stretched below us like a chess board. Here and there where had been houses were now but piles of ruins. The lines here were quite far apart—perhaps half a mile, and in between them were acres of land under cultivation. I think that the most remarkable thing that I have seen in this war was the sight of peasants working between the lines as calmly as though no such thing as war existed. Through the glasses I could distinctly see one old white beard with a horse ploughing up a field, and even as I was looking at him I saw a shell burst not half a mile beyond him near one of the German positions. I mentioned it to one of the officers. "Oh yes," he said, "neither we nor the Germans fire on the peasants nowadays. They must do their work and they harm neither of us."

On this part of the line the war seems to have become rather a listless affair and perfunctory to say the least. I suppose both Germans and Russians have instructions just now to hold themselves on the defensive. At any rate I could distinctly see movements beyond the German line, and I am sure they too must have detected the same on our side. One man on a white horse was clearly visible as he rode along behind the German trenches, while I followed with my glasses a German motor-car that sped down a road leaving in its wake a cloud of dust. Yet no one bothered much about either of them. Now and again one of our big guns behind us would thunder, and over our heads we could hear the diminishing wail of a 15-centimetre shell as it sped on its journey to the German lines. Through the hyperscope one could clearly see the clouds of dirt and dust thrown up by the explosion. One of these shells fell squarely in one of the German trenches, and as the smoke drifted away I could not help wondering how many poor wretches had been torn by its fragments. After watching this performance for an hour or more, we returned back through the trench and paid a visit to the Colonel in his abode in the earth by the roadside. For half an hour or more we chatted with him and then bade him good-bye.

A bit to the south-west of us lay a town which a few days ago was shelled by the Germans. This town lies in a salient of our line, and since the bombardment has been abandoned by all the population. As it lay on the German side of the slope we had three miles of exposed roadway to cover to get to it, and another three miles in view of the German line to get out of it.

Russian General inspecting his gunners.

As we sped down this three miles one felt a certain satisfaction that one had a 95 horsepower Napier capable of doing 80 miles an hour. A third of the town itself was destroyed by the German shell fire. The rest was like a city of the dead. Not a human being of the population was to be seen in the streets, which but a week ago were swarming with people. Here and there a soldier from the near-by positions lounged on an abandoned doorstep, or napped peacefully under one of the trees in the square. The sun of noon looked down upon a deserted village, if one does not count an occasional dog prowling about, or one white kitty sitting calmly on a window ledge in the sunshine casually washing her face. As ruins have long ceased to attract us, we did not loiter long here, but turned eastward along the great white road that led back in the direction of Warsaw.

There is one strip of this road which I suppose is not more than 4,500 yards from the German gun positions. Personally I am always interested in these matters, and being of an inquiring turn of mind I asked my friend the Russian officer, who was with me in the car, if he thought the enemy could see us. "Oh yes," he replied quite cheerfully. "I am sure they can see us, but I don't think they can hit us. Probably they won't try, as they are not wasting ammunition as much as they used to. Won't you have a cigarette?" I accepted the smoke gladly and concluded that it is the Russian custom to offer one a cigarette every time one asks this question about the German guns. Anyway, I got exactly the same reply from this man as I did from the other in the morning.

Ten miles up the road we came on a bit of forest where the unfortunate villagers who had been driven out by shell fire were camping. Here they were in the wood living in rude lean-to's, surrounded by all their worldly possessions that they had the means of getting away. Cows, ducks, pigs, and chicken roamed about the forests, while dozens of children played about in the dust.

One picture I shall not forget. Before a hut made of straw and branches of trees a mother had constructed a rude oven in the earth by setting on some stones the steel top of the kitchen stove that she had brought with her. Kneeling over the fire she was preparing the primitive noonday meal. Just behind was a cradle in which lay a few weeks' old baby rocked by a little sister of four. Three other little children stood expectantly around the fire, their little mouths watering for the crude meal that was in preparation. Behind the cradle lay the family cow, her soft brown eyes gazing mournfully at the cradle as she chewed reflectively at her cud. In the door of the miserable little shelter stretched a great fat sow sleeping sweetly with her lips twitching nervously in her sleep. An old hen with a dozen chicks was clucking to her little brood within the open end of the hut. This was all that war had left of one home.

Telephoning to the battery from the observation position.

A hundred yards away a gang of labourers was digging in the forest. It is no wonder that the mother looks nervously from her fire at their work. Perhaps she wonders what they are about. We know. It is another line of trenches. From what we have seen of the front line we believe they will not be needed, but it is not strange that these poor fugitives look on with anxious eyes with the question written large on every face. Probably to them the war seems something from which they cannot escape. They came to this wood for safety and now again they see more digging of trenches going on.

Another hour on the road brings us back to the head-quarters of the army and our day in May is over.

CHAPTER VIII
THE CHANGE OF FRONT IN POLAND AND THE BATTLE OF OPATOV

Dated:
OPATOV, POLAND,
May 31, 1915.

FOR the last three days I have been with a certain army of the Russians that occupies the strip of Poland between the Pilitza river and the Vistula on the south. I feel intense regret that the restrictions of the censor proscribe the identification of military units or of their definite location. These wonderful corps, divisions and battalions should, in my view, have all the honour that is their due, but the writer can only abide by the wishes of the authorities by whose kindness and courtesy he has been able to visit these positions.

Leaving Warsaw in a motor car in the evening, and running until an early hour in the morning, we found ourselves the next day at the head-quarters of one of the really great army commanders of Russia. With him and the members of his staff we spent the chief part of the morning, when every opportunity was given us to study the situation within his jurisdiction. To go to the Front, as I have often written before, means a two to three days' trip, and the inspection of a single detail of the vast operations that have been conducted. At the suggestion of the Commander we decided to visit a certain army corps in the south, whose success in the operations attending the change of front had been so extraordinary, that everyone at the staff was filled with pride and eager to have its work appreciated. Before going on to describe the work of this particular corps it is proper to mention a little more particularly the work of this one army as a whole since the beginning of the war.

This army stood before Lublin during the crisis in the early days of the war, and by uniting with that of Plevie, and the two joining with Russky to the east of them, there resulted the first great crash to the Austrian arms in Galicia. Later, this same army came back north and was engaged in the terrific fighting around Ivangorod, which resulted in the defeat of the enemy and their expulsion from Poland last autumn.

In the advance after the taking back of Radom and Kielce, the army came under the very walls of Cracow, and in all of its divisions and brigades there was scarcely a battalion that did not distinguish itself in that terrific fighting. When the Germans began their second invasion of Poland last autumn, this army regretfully fell back to its positions on the Nida river, and when the last storm broke in Galicia and the retirement of the army of the Dunajec rendered a change of the Russian-Polish line a strategic necessity, the army with all its numerous corps was again called upon to fall back in order that the Front as a whole might be a symmetrical one.

During this change of front we heard a great deal in Warsaw, from people who delight in circulating false stories, of Russian disasters in Southern Poland. I have been particularly interested, therefore, in checking up this movement on the ground and getting at the actual facts of the case. As a fact, the Russian retirement was made amid the lamentations and grumbling of the whole army. The private soldiers, who do not follow strategy very closely, complained bitterly that they, who had never met defeat, and before whom the enemy had always fallen back when they attacked, should be called upon to retreat when they were sure, regiment by regiment, that they could beat twice their numbers of the enemy. The Germans and Austrians advanced with great caution for several days. Knowing, however, the location of the new Russian line, they imagined that their adversaries would fall back on it in a few big marches and await them there. Besides this, both Germans and Austrians had been carefully fed with reports of the Galician movement to the effect that the Russians were retiring in utter defeat, that even in Poland they were panic-stricken and would probably put up but a feeble fight even on their line.

I could not in the brief time which I had for this trip visit all the corps involved in this movement, and at the suggestion of the General of the army, visited only the — corps, whose operations may be regarded as typical of the whole spirit in which this front was changed. Regarding the movement as a whole it is sufficient to say that in the two weeks following the change of line in Poland, the corps comprising this one army made the enemy suffer losses, in killed, wounded and prisoners, which the General estimated at nearly 30,000, of whom about 9,000 were prisoners. All of this was done at a comparatively trifling loss to the Russians themselves. From which very brief summary of the change of front it will be realized that this particular army has neither lost its fighting spirit nor has its *moral* suffered from the retirement to another line.

In the trenches near Opatov.

There are so many big movements in this war that it is utterly impossible for one observer to describe more than a trifling fraction of the achievements that are made here. Since the General Staff have given me what appears to be a free range in the north-eastern armies, I have had so many interesting opportunities that it is difficult to pick any one in preference to another. What I am writing in this story is merely the narrative of a single corps during this change of front, and I think it a significant story, because I believe it typifies not only the corps of this particular army, but practically all the corps now in the field on this Front. General Ragosa, who commands this corps, and who has entertained me for the best part of three days, has given me every opportunity to study his whole movement and permitted one of his officers to prepare sketches, illustrating his movement. The General himself, like most men who deal with big affairs, is a very modest and simple man. To talk with him one would not guess that the movement which has resulted so successfully for his corps and so disastrously for the enemy, was the product of a programme worked out in the quiet of a remote head-quarters and carried successfully through under his direction by means of the field wire stretched through the forest for the 30 kilometres that separate his head-quarters from the fighting line.

When I suggested to him that his fighting around Opatov made an extremely interesting story, he only shrugged his shoulders and replied, "But in this war it is only a small fight. What is the operation of a single army, much less the work of one of its units?" Yet one feels that the success of this war will be the sum of the work of the many units, and as this battle resulted in the entire breaking up of the symmetry of the Austro-German following movement, and is one of the few actions during the recent months of this war which was fought in the open without trenches, it is extremely interesting. Indeed, in any other war it would have been called a good-sized action; from first to last on both sides I suppose that more than 100,000 men and perhaps 350 to 400 guns were engaged. Let me describe it.

General Ragosa's corps was on the Nida river, and it was with great regret that the troops left the trenches that they had been defending all winter. Their new line was extremely strong, and after they had started, it was assumed by the enemy that they could leisurely follow the Russians, and again sit down before their positions.

Second-line trenches, Opatov.

But they were not counting on this particular General when they made their advance. Instead of going back to his line, he brought his units to the line running from Lubenia to and through Opatov to the south, where he halted and awaited the advancing enemy who came on in four divisions. These were the third German Landwehr division who were moving eastward and a little to the north of Lubenia. Next, coming from the direction of Kielce was the German division of General Bredow supported by the 84th Austrian regiment; this unit was moving directly against the manufacturing town of Ostzowiec. Further to the south came the crack Austrian division, the 25th, which was composed of the 4th Deutschmeister regiment from Vienna and the 25th, 17th and 10th Jäger units, the division itself being commanded by the Archduke Peter Ferdinand. The 25th division was moving on the Lagow road headed for Opatov, while the 4th Austrian division (a Landwehr formation) supported by the 41st Honved division (regiments 20, 31, 32 and one other) was making for the same objective. It is probable that the enemy units, approaching the command of Ragosa, outnumbered the Russians in that particular portion of the theatre of operations by at least forty per cent. Certainly they never expected that any action would be given by the supposedly demoralized Russians short of their fortified line, to which they were supposed by the enemy to be retiring in hot haste.

General Ragosa wishing to finish up the weakest portion first, as usual picked the Austrians for his first surprise party. But this action he anticipated by making a feint against the German corps, driving in their advance guards by vigorous attacks and causing the whole movement to halt and commence deploying for an engagement. This took place on May 15. On the same day with all his available strength he swung furiously, with Opatov as an axis from both north and south, catching the 25th division on the road between Lagow and Opatov with a bayonet charge delivered from the mountain over and around which his troops had been marching all night. Simultaneously another portion of his command swept up on the 4th division coming from Iwaniska to Opatov. In the meantime a heavy force of Cossacks had ridden round the Austrian line and actually hit their line of communications at the exact time that the infantry fell on the main column with a bayonet charge of such impetuosity and fury that the entire Austrian formation crumpled up.

At the same time the 4th division was meeting a similar fate further south; the two were thrown together in a helpless mass and suffered a loss of between three and four thousand in casualties and nearly three thousand in prisoners, besides losing a large number of machine guns and the bulk of their baggage. The balance, supported by the 41st Honved division, which had been hurried up, managed to wriggle themselves out of their predicament by falling back on Wokacow, and the whole retired to Lagow, beyond which the Russians were not permitted to pursue them lest they should break the symmetry of their own entire line. Immediately after this action against the Austrians, a large portion of the same troops made a forced march back over the mountain which had separated the Austrians from their German neighbours and fell on the right of the German formation, while the frontal attacks, which had formerly been feints, were now delivered in dead earnest.

The result was that Bredow's formation was taken suddenly in front and on its right flank, and on May 18 began to fall back until it was supported by the 4th Landwehr division, which had been hurriedly snatched out of the line to the north to prevent Bredow from suffering a fate similar to that which overtook the Austrians to the south. After falling back to Bodzentin where it was joined by the supports from the north, the Germans pulled themselves together to make a stand. But here, as in the south, general orders prevented the Russians from moving further against their defeated foe lest in their enthusiasm they might advance too far and leave a hole in their own line. Thus Ragosa's command after four days of constant action came to a stand and their part in the movement ended.

But the trouble of the enemy was not over. Ragosa at once discovered that the 4th Landwehr division that had been hurried up to support retreating Bredow, had been taken from the front of his neighbouring corps, and this information he promptly passed on to his friend commanding the — corps who gladly passed the word on to his own front. The regiments in that quarter promptly punched a hole in the German weakened line, and with vicious bayonet attacks killed and captured a large number of Germans, also forcing back their line. Something similar happened in the corps to the south of Ragosa's corps who were in a fever of excitement because of the big fighting on the San, which was going on just to their left while Ragosa's guns were thundering just to the north. The result was that out of a kind of sympathetic contagion, they fixed bayonets and rushed on the enemy in their front with a fury equal to that which was going on in both corps north of them. Thus it came about that three quarters of this particular army became engaged in general action by the sheer initiative of Ragosa, and maintained it entirely by the enthusiasm of the troops engaged. These corps even in retreat could not be restrained from going back and having a turn with the enemy.

A second-line trench near Opatov.

The change of front in Poland resulted in losses in killed, wounded and prisoners to the enemy, approximating in this army alone between 20,000 and 30,000, with a loss to the Russians probably less than a third of that number, besides resulting in an increase of *moral* to the latter, which has fully offset any depression caused by their retirement. In talking with their officers, and I talked with at least a score, I heard everywhere the same complaint, namely that it was becoming increasingly difficult to keep their soldiers in the trenches. So eager is the whole army to be advancing, that only constant discipline and watching prevent individual units from becoming excited and getting up and attacking, thus precipitating a general action which the Russians wish to avoid while the movement in Galicia is one of fluctuation and uncertainty.

Little definite information was available on this Front as to what was going on further south, but certainly I found not the slightest sign of depression among either men or officers with whom I talked. As one remarked, "Well, what of it? You do not understand our soldiers. They can retreat every day for a month and come back as full of fight at the end of that time as when they started. A few Russian 'defeats,' as the Germans call them, will be a disaster for the Kaiser. Don't worry. We will come back all right and it cannot be too soon for the taste of this army."

CHAPTER IX
WITH THE ARMY IN SOUTHERN POLAND

Dated:

A Certain Army Corps Head-quarters
Somewhere in Southern Poland
June 1, 1915.

TO-DAY has been one of the most interesting that I have spent since I came to Russia last September. The General commanding this certain army corps, which, while the war lasts, must not be identified, carefully mapped out an ideal day for us, and made it possible of fulfilment by placing two motors at our disposal and permitting a member of his personal staff to accompany us as guide, philosopher and friend. This very charming gentleman, M. Riabonschisky, represents a type which one sees increasingly in the Russian Army as the war grows older. M. Riabonschisky served his term of years in the army, and then being wealthy and of a distinguished Moscow family, went into the banking business, and the beginning of the war found him one of the leading business men of the old Russian capital. With the first call he instantly abandoned his desk and sedentary habits, and became again a subaltern, which was his rank twenty odd years ago; when he came to the Front it was as aide-de-camp of a General commanding an army corps.

In a shabby uniform and with face tanned to the colour of old leather one now finds the Moscow millionaire working harder than a common soldier. Our friend had by no means confined his activities to routine work at head-quarters, but as the St. George's Cross on his breast indicated, had seen a bit of active service as well. Though he talked freely enough on every known subject, I found him uncommunicative on the subject of his Cross denoting distinguished merit in the face of an enemy. A little persistent tact, however, finally got out of him that before Lublin, in a crisis on the positions, he had gone to the front line trenches in a motor car loaded with ammunition for the troops who for lack of it were on the point of retiring. With the return trip he brought out all the wounded his car could hold. This, then, was the former banker who now accompanied us on a tour of inspection of the army of which he was as proud as the Commanding General himself was.

A Russian first-line trench near Lublin.

The companion picture shows the German position through loop-hole.

German position near Lublin.

Photo taken through loop-hole in trench.

Leaving our head-quarters we drove south through a beautiful woodland for nearly two hours, to the headquarters of that certain division of the army which has covered itself with glory in the recent fighting around Opatov, where we were received cordially by the commander. Telegrams sent ahead had advised him of our arrival, and he had done his part in arranging details that our trip might be as interesting as possible. After a few minutes drinking tea and smoking cigarettes we again took cars and motored for another 16 versts to the town of Opatov, where one of the brigade head-quarters was located. This quaint old Polish town with a castle and a wall around it has been three times visited by the tide of battle, and the hills about it (it lies in a hollow) are pitted with the caves made by the uneasy inhabitants, whose experience of shell fire has been disturbing. One imagines from the number of dugouts one sees that the whole population might easily move under ground at an hour's notice. However, in spite of the tumult of battles which have been fought around it, Opatov has not been scarred by shell fire.

From here we went directly west on the road to Lagow for perhaps 5 versts, when we turned off suddenly on to a faint road and down into a little hollow where a tiny village nestled in which we were told we should find the head-quarters of a certain regiment that we had come to visit. As our cars came over the crest of the hill we noticed assembled on a flat field, that lay in the hollow, absolutely concealed from the outside world, a block of troops standing under arms. My first impression was that this was a couple of reserve units just going back to the trenches to relieve their fellows. We were delighted at such a bit of luck. On pulling up our cars by the side of the road we found ourselves greeted by the Colonel and staff of the regiment, to whom we were introduced by our guide. After a few words in Russian my friend turned, his face wreathed in smiles, and said, "The Colonel is very kind; he has ordered a review for your inspection."

With the staff we strolled up to the centre of the field, where on two sides we faced two of the most magnificent battalions of troops that it has ever been my fortune to see, while on the third side were parked the machine-gun batteries of the regiment. For a few minutes we stood in the centre of the three-sided square while the Colonel, with unconcealed pride, told us something of the history of the regiment that stood before us. Its name and its corps must not be mentioned, but it is permissible to say that it is from Moscow and is one of the oldest regiments in the Russian service, with traditions running back for 125 years. It is one of the two formations of the entire Russian army which is permitted to march in review with fixed bayonets, a distinction acquired by 125 years of history marked by successful work with cold steel.

March-past of the Gonogoriski Regiment.

I have written in a previous chapter of the fighting around Opatov and of the wonderful work done by the troops of this army corps. Now we learned from the Colonel that it was his regiment that made the march over the mountain, and fell with the bayonet upon the flank of the 25th Austrian division with such an impetus and fury that every man had killed or captured a soldier of the enemy. That we might not minimize the glory of his men the Colonel assured us that the Austrian 25th was no scrub Landwehr or reserve formation, but the very élite of the élite of the Austrian army, embodying the famous Deutschmeister regiment from Vienna, which was supposed to be the finest organization of infantry in the Hapsburg realm. What we saw before us were two of the four battalions of the Moscow regiment who were in reserve for a few days' rest, while their brothers in the other two battalions were 4 versts forward in the fighting line.

Suddenly the Colonel turned about and in a voice of thunder uttered a command, and instantly the two thousand men became as rigid as two thousand statues. Another word, and with the click of a bit of well-oiled mechanism, two thousand rifles came to the present. Another command from the Colonel and the regimental band on the right flank, with its thirty pieces of brass, burst forth with "Rule Britannia." A moment's silence followed, and then came the strains of the American National Anthem, followed in turn by the Russian National Anthem.

As the last strain died away there came another sharp command from the Colonel, and once more the mechanism clicked and two thousand guns came to the ground as one. Then, stepping out from the little group of the staff, the Colonel addressed the regiment in a deep melodious voice in words that carried to the furthest man. I have written much of the rapidly growing feeling of friendship and affection between England and Russia. For six months I have noticed a gradual development of this sentiment, but I have never realized until this day that it was percolating to the very foundations of the Russian people. In Petrograd and Moscow one naturally expects the diplomats and politicians to emphasize this point to a member of the press. But out at the Front these men who deal in steel and blood are not given to fine phrases, nor are they wont to speak for effect. For ten months their lives have been lives of danger and hardships, and in their eyes and in their faces one sees sincerity and truth written large for those who study human nature to read. The speech was to me so impressive that it seems well worth while to quote the officer's stirring words, words which found an echo in the heart of the writer, who is an American citizen and not a British subject at all. With his hand held aloft the Colonel said:—

Men of the Gonogoriski Regiment cheering King George V.

"Attention,—Gentlemen, officers and soldiers: We have to-day the honour to receive the representatives of the great English nation, our faithful allies now fighting with us for the good of us all to punish our common treacherous enemy. They are dear to our hearts because they are conducting this war with such sacrifices and such incredible bravery. It is a great pleasure and privilege for our regiment to see among us the representatives of the country where dwell the bravest of the brave. This regiment, beloved of Suvoroff, will always do its uttermost to uphold the reputation of Russian arms, that they may be worthy to fight this battle shoulder to shoulder with their noble allies in the British army. Officers and soldiers, I call for a hearty cheer for the great King of England. Long live George the Fifth."

The response came from two thousand lungs and throats with the suddenness of a clap of thunder. Out of the misery and chaos of this world-disaster there is surely coming a new spirit and a new-found feeling of respect and regard between the allied nations, a feeling which in itself is perhaps laying the foundation of a greater peace movement than all the harangues and platitudes of the preachers of pacificism. Before this war I dare say that England and the English meant nothing to the peasant soldier of Russia. This is no longer true, and to stand as I stood in this hollow square and listen for five minutes to these war-stained veterans cheering themselves hoarse for the ally whom they have been taught to consider the personification of soldierly virtues, was to feel that perhaps from this war may come future relations which the next generation will look back upon as having in large measure justified the price. The Colonel raised his hand and instantly the tumult died away. The Colonel courteously invited me to address the Regiment on behalf of England, but as a neutral this was an impossible role.

Men of the Gonogoriski Regiment.

Afterwards the Colonel ordered a review of the two battalions, and in company formation they passed by with their bayonets at the charge and with every eye fixed on the commander, while every officer marched at the salute. I have never seen a more impressive body of men. Dirty and shabby, with faces tanned like shoe leather, and unshaven, they marched past, the picture of men of action. In each face was the pride of regiment and country and the respect of self. As they passed, company after company, the beaming Colonel said to me, "When my men come at the charge the Austrians never wait for them to come into the trenches. They fire on us until we are within ten feet and then they fall on their knees and beg for quarter." As the writer looked into these earnest serious faces that passed by, each seamed with lines of grim determination and eyes steeled with the hardness engendered by war, he felt an increased respect for the Austrian who waited until the enemy were within ten feet. Somehow one felt that a hundred feet start would be an insufficient handicap to get away from these fellows when they came for one with their bayonets levelled and their leather throats howling for the blood of the enemy.

After the infantry we inspected the machine-gun batteries of the regiment, and with special pride the Colonel showed us the four captured machine-guns taken from the Austrians in the recent action, together with large quantities of ammunition. After the machine-guns were examined, the heroes of the St. George's Cross, decorated in the recent battle, were brought forward to be photographed. Then the band played the air of the regiment, while the officers of the regiment joined in singing a rousing melody which has been the regimental song for the 125 years of its existence. Then, preceded by the band, we went to the Colonel's head-quarters, where lunch was served, the band playing outside while we ate.

The head-quarters of the Colonel were in a schoolhouse hurriedly adapted to the needs of war. Our table was the children's blackboard taken from the walls and stretched between two desks, the scholars' benches serving us in lieu of chairs. The only thing in the whole establishment that did not reek of the necessities of war was the food, which was excellent. The rugged Colonel, lean as a race horse and as tough as whipcord, may in some former life when he was in Moscow have been an epicure and something of a good liver. Anyway the cooking was perfection.

In conversation with a number of the men who sat at table, I heard that their regiment had been in thirty-four actions since the war had started. The Colonel himself had been wounded no less than three times in the war. One Captain of the staff showed me a hat with a bullet hole in the top made in the last battle; while the Lieutenant-Colonel laughingly told me that they could not kill him at all; though he received seventeen bullets through his clothes since the war started he had never been scratched in any action in which he had been engaged. The tactical position of a Colonel in the Russian army is in the rear, I am told, but in this regiment I learned from one of the officers, the Colonel rarely was in the rear, and on more than one occasion he had led the charge at the very head of his men.

CHAPTER X
AN AFTERNOON AT THE "POSITIONS"

Dated:

SOMEWHERE IN POLAND,
June 2, 1915.

PROVIDED with carriages we left our hospitable Colonel for the front trenches 4 versts further on. As we were near the Front when we were at regimental head-quarters it was not deemed safe to take the motor-cars any further, on account of the clouds of dust which they leave in their wake.

The country here is spread out in great rolling valleys with very little timber and only occasional crests or ridges separating one beautiful verdant stretch of landscape from another. It struck one as quite obvious in riding over this country that the men who planned these roads had not taken war into consideration. Had they done so they certainly would not have placed them so generally along ridges, where one's progress can be seen from about 10 versts in every direction. As I have mentioned in an earlier chapter, this particular army had not fallen back on its fortified and prepared line, but was camping out about 25 to 30 versts in front of it in positions which were somewhat informal. In riding through this country one has the unpleasant sensation that every time one shows up on a ridge, an enemy of an observing and enterprising disposition might be tempted to take a shot at one just for practice. My friend the banker soldier explained, however, that we should be difficult to hit, and anyway he rather enjoyed shell fire. "It is a sort of nice game," he told me with a charming smile, "one finds it very entertaining and not altogether dangerous."

However his insouciance did not prevent him taking the precaution of forbidding the use of motor-cars with their clouds of dust, and he was quite content that we should take the carriages, which made less of a target on the dry roads.

From regimental head-quarters we went up into a little gulch where we again found that we were expected, and a genial Colonel of a howitzer battery was waiting to entertain us. Five of our guns were sitting along the road with their muzzled noses up in the air at an angle of about 35 degrees waiting, waiting for some one to give them word to shoot at something or other.

Howitzer battery in Poland.

Batteries are always peculiarly fascinating to me; they always appear so perfect in their efficiency, and capable of getting work done when required. These five were of the 4-inch variety, with an elevation of forty-five degrees obtainable.

At a word from the Colonel they were cleared for action and their sighting apparatus inspected and explained. As usual they were equipped with panorama sights, with the aiming point a group of trees to the right and rear of the position, and with their observation point 3 miles away in a trench near the infantry line. The sixth gun was doing lonely duty a mile away in a little trench all by itself. This position the Colonel informed us was shelled yesterday by the enemy, who fired thirty-five 12-centimetre shells at them without scoring a single hit. After looking at the guns we spent an hour at tea, and then in our carts pushed on up the valley, where we found a regiment of Cossack cavalry in reserve. The hundreds of horses were all saddled and wandering about, each meandering where its fancy led. Everywhere on the grass and under the few clumps of brush were sitting or sleeping the men, few of whom had any shelter or tents of any kind, and the whole encampment was about as informal as the encampment of a herd of cattle. In fact the Cossacks impress one as a kind of game who have no more need of shelter or comforts than the deer of the forest. When they settle down for the night they turn their horses loose, eat a bit of ration and then sit under a tree and go to sleep. It is all very charming and simple. Our guide informed us that when they wanted their horses they simply went out and whistled for them as a mother sheep bleats for its young, and that in a surprisingly short time every soldier found his mount. The soldiers are devoted to their horses, and in a dozen different places one could see them rubbing down their mounts or rubbing their noses and petting them.

From this encampment the road went up to its usual place on the crest of the hill. The soldier driver of our carriage did not seem to feel the same amount of enthusiasm about the "nice game" of being shelled, and protested as much as he dared about taking the horses further; but being quietly sat upon, he subsided with a deep sigh and started up over the ridge in the direction of a clump of houses beyond another rise of ground at an astonishingly rapid speed. From the crest along which we travelled we had a beautiful view of a gently undulating valley lying peaceful and serene under the warm afternoon sun. A few insects buzzing about in the soft air near the carriage were the only signs of life about us. We drove up at a good round pace to the little clump of trees which sheltered a group of farm buildings. As we were getting out of our carriage there was a sharp report to the road on our right, and looking back I saw the fleecy white puff of a shrapnel shell breaking just over the road to the north of us. Like the bloom of cotton the smoke hung for an instant in the air and then slowly expanding drifted off. A moment later, almost in the same place, another beautiful white puff, with its heart of copper-red, appeared over the road, and again the sharp sound of its burst drifted across the valley. The Austrian shrapnel has a bit of reddish-brown smoke which must be, I think, from the bursting charge in the shell.

Cossacks on the Dniester. Officers' quarters in the woods.

Our guide was quite delighted and smiled and clicked his heels cheerfully as he ushered us into the little room of the officer commanding the regiment in the trenches just ahead of us. Even as he greeted us, the telephone rang in the little low-ceilinged room of the cottage, and he excused himself as he went to reply to it. In a few minutes he came back with an annoyed expression on his face. "These unpleasant Austrians," he said in disgust. "They are always up to their silly tricks. They have been shelling some Red Cross carts on the road. I have just ordered the howitzer battery in our rear to come into action and we shall see if we cannot give them a lesson in manners."

After a few pleasantries he asked what it was that we would most like, and I replied in my stock phrases, "Observation points and trenches, if you please." He stood for a moment studying the tip of his dusty boot; evidently he was not very eager about the job. However, he shrugged his shoulders and went back to the telephone, and after a few minutes conversation came back and said to us: "It is a very bad time to go into our trenches, as we have no covered ways, and in the daytime one is seen, and the enemy always begin firing. It is very unsafe, but if you are very anxious I shall permit one of you to go forward, though it is not convenient. When the enemy begin to fire, our batteries reply, and firing starts in all the trenches. The soldiers like to fight, and it doesn't take much to start them."

Put in this way none of us felt very keen about insisting. So we all compromised by a visit to a secondary position, which we were told was not very dangerous, as the enemy could only reach it with their shell fire and "of course no one minds that," as the officer casually put it. We all agreed that, of course, we did not mind that, and so trooped off with the Colonel to the trenches and dug-outs where the troops who were not in the firing line were in immediate reserve.

The group of dug-outs was flanked with trenches, for, as the Colonel informed us, "Who knows when this position may be attacked?" And then he added, "You see, though we are not in the direct view of the enemy here, they know our whereabouts and usually about this time of day they shell the place. They can reach it very nicely and from two different directions. Yesterday it became so hot in our house that we all spent a quiet afternoon in the dug-outs." He paused and offered us a cigarette, and as he did so there came a deep boom from our rear and a howitzer shell wailed over our heads on its mission of protest to the Austrians about firing on Red Cross wagons. A few seconds later the muffled report of its explosion came back across the valley. A second later another and another shell went over our heads. The Colonel smiled, "You see," he said, "my orders are being carried out. No doubt the enemy will reply soon."

His belief was justified. A moment later that extremely distressing sound made by an approaching shell came to our ears, followed immediately by its sharp report as it burst in a field a few hundred yards away. I looked about at the soldiers and officers around me, but not one even cast a glance in the direction of the smoke drifting away over the field near by. After wandering about his position for half or three-quarters of an hour, we returned to the cottage. It consisted of but three rooms. The telephone room, a little den where the officers ate, and a large room filled with straw on which they slept at night, when sleeping was possible.

Here we met a fine grey-haired, grizzled Colonel, who, as my banker friend informed me, commanded a neighbouring regiment, the — Grenadiers. He is one of our finest officers and is in every way worthy of his regiment, the history of which stretches back over two centuries. The officer himself looked tired and shabby, and his face was deeply lined with furrows. We read about dreadful sacrifices in the Western fighting, but I think this regiment, which again I regret that I cannot name, has suffered as much in this war as any unit on any Front. In the two weeks of fighting around Cracow alone it has dwindled from 4,000 men to 800, and that fortnight represented but a small fraction of the campaigning which it has done since the war started. Again and again it has been filled to its full strength, and after every important action its ranks were depleted hideously. Now there are very few left of the original members, but as an officer proudly said, "These regiments have their traditions of which their soldiers are proud. Put a moujik in its uniform and to-morrow he is a grenadier and proud of it."

The Colonel, who sat by the little table as we talked, did not speak English, but in response to the question of a friend who addressed him in Russian, he said with a tired little smile, "Well, yes, after ten months one is getting rather tired of the war. One hopes it will soon be over and that one may see one's home and children once more, but one wonders if——" He paused, smiled a little, and offered us a cigarette. It is not strange that these men who live day and night so near the trenches that they are never out of sound of firing, and never sleep out of the zone of bursting shells, whose every day is associated with friends and soldiers among the fallen, wonder vaguely if they will ever get home. The trench occupied by this man's command was so exposed that he could only reach it unobserved by crawling on his stomach over the ridge, and into the shallow ditch that served his troops for shelter.

Leaving the little farm we drove back over the road above which we had seen the bursting shells on our arrival, but our own batteries, no doubt, had diverted the enemy from practice on the road, for we made the 3 versts without a single one coming our way.

It was closing twilight when we started back for the head-quarters that we had left in the early morning. The sun had set and the peace and serenity of the evening were broken only by the distant thunder of an occasional shell bursting in the west. From the ridge over which our road ran I could distinctly see the smoke from three different burning villages fired by the German artillery. One wonders what on earth the enemy have in mind when they deliberately shell these pathetic little patches of straw-thatched peasant homes. Even in ordinary times these people seem to have a hard life in making both ends meet, but now in the war their lot is a most wretched one. Apparently hardly a day passes that some village is not burned by the long range shells of the enemy's guns. That such action has any military benefit seems unlikely. The mind of the enemy seems bent on destruction, and everywhere their foot is placed grief follows.

The next morning for several hours I chatted with the General and his Chief of Staff, and found, as always at the Front, the greatest optimism. "Have you seen our soldiers at the Front?" is the question always asked, and when one answers in the affirmative they say, "Well, then how can you have any anxiety as to the future. These men may retire a dozen times, but demoralized or discouraged they are never. We shall win absolutely surely. Do not doubt it."

The Polish Legion.

One forms the opinion that the place for the pessimist is at the Front. In the crises one leaves the big cities in a cloud of gloom, and the enthusiasm and spirit increase steadily, until in the front trenches one finds the officers exercising every effort to keep their men from climbing out of their shelters and going across the way and bayoneting the enemy. The morale of the Russian Army as I have seen it in these last weeks is extraordinary.

We left head-quarters and motored over wretched roads to the little town of Ilza where the quaintest village I have seen lies in a little hollow beneath a hill on which is perched the old ruin of a castle, its crumbling ramparts and decaying battlements standing silhouetted against the sky. We halted in the village to inquire the condition of the road to Radom, for the day we came this way the enemy had been shelling it and the remains of a horse scattered for 50 feet along the highway told us that their practice was not bad at all. We were informed that the artillery of the Germans commanded the first 4 versts, but after that it was safe enough. Somehow no one feels much apprehension about artillery fire, and in our speedy car we felt confident enough of doing the 4 versts in sufficient haste to make the chance of a shot hitting us at 6,500 yards a very slight one. As soon as we came out of the hollow, and along the great white road which stretched across the green fields, I saw one of the great sausage-shaped German Zeppelins hanging menacingly in the sky to the west of us. It was a perfectly still day and the vessel seemed quite motionless.

At the end of the 4 versts mentioned there was a long hill, and then the road dipped out of sight into another valley where the omniscient eye of the German sausage could not follow us. It was in my own mind that it would not be unpleasant when we crossed the ridge. We were just beginning the climb of the hill when our own motor-car (which had been coughing and protesting all day) gave three huge snorts, exploded three times in the engine, and came to a dead stop on the road, with that indescribable expression on its snubby inanimate nose of a car that had finished for the day. The part of the road that we were on was as white as chalk against the green of the hill, with only a few skinny trees (at least they certainly looked skinny to me) to hide us. Frantic efforts to crank the car and get it started only resulted in a few explosions, and minor protests from its interior.

So there we sat in the blazing sun while our extremely competent chauffeur took off his coat and crawled under the car and did a lot of tinkering and hammering. He was such a good and cool-headed individual and went about his work so conscientiously that one did not feel inclined to go off in the one good car and leave him alone in his predicament. So we all sat under the skinny tree and smoked while we watched three shells burst on the road over which we had just passed. I must confess to a feeling of extreme annoyance at this particular moment. One can feel a certain exaltation in hustling down a road at seventy miles an hour and being shot at, but somehow there is very little interest in sitting out in the blazing sun on a white road hoping that you can get your car started before the enemy gets your range. About the time the third shell landed on the road, our car changed its mind and its engines suddenly went into action with a tumult like a machine gun battery. We climbed in our cars and the driver threw in the clutches and our motor made at least fifty feet in one jump and went over the crest of the hill in a cloud of dust. The man who sold it to me assured me that it once did 140 versts on a race track in one hour. My own impression is that it was doing about 150 an hour when it cleared the ridge and the Zeppelin was lost to sight.

An hour later we were in Radom, and by midnight back once more in Warsaw.

CHAPTER XI
HOW THE RUSSIANS MET THE FIRST GAS ATTACK

Dated:
ZYRARDOW, POLAND,
June 5, 1915.

ONE of the finest stories of fortitude and heroism that the war on this front has produced is of how the Siberian troops met the first large scale attack upon their lines in which the enemy made use of the gas horror, that latest product of the ingenuity of the Germans who boast so loudly and so continuously of their *kultur* and the standards of civilization and humanity which they declare it is their sacred duty to force upon the world.

There has been a lull in the fighting on this immediate front for some time, due to the fact that the Germans have diverted all the troops that they could safely spare to strengthen their concentration in Galicia. Only an occasional spasm of fighting with bursts of artillery firing, first in one point and then another, have created sufficient incident to mark one day from another. During this time the reports of the use of poisoned gases and shells containing deadly fumes have drifted over to this side, and it has been expected that sooner or later something of the same sort would be experienced on the Bzura front. Many times we have had shells containing formaline fumes and other noxious poisons sent screaming over our trenches, but their use heretofore seemed rather in the nature of an experiment than of a serious innovation. Enough, however, has been said about them here, and when the effort on a wholesale scale was made, it found our troops prepared morally, if not yet with actual equipment in the way of respirators.

The first battle of the gases occurred early on the morning of Sunday, the 30th of May. The days are very long here now, and the first pale streaks of grey were just tinging the western horizon, when the look-outs in the Russian trenches on the Bzura discovered signs of activity in the trenches of the enemy which at this point are not very far away from our lines. War has become such an every-day business that an impending attack creates no more excitement in the trenches than a doctor feels when he is called out at night to visit a patient. Word was passed down the trenches to the sleeping soldiers, who at once crawled out of their shelters and dug-outs, and rubbing their sleepy eyes took their places at the loopholes and laid out, ready for use, their piles of cartridge clips. The machine gun operators uncovered their guns and looked to them to see that all was well oiled and working smoothly, while the officers strolled about the trenches with words of advice and encouragement to their men.

Back in the reserve trenches the soldiers were turning out more leisurely in response to the alarm telephoned back. Regimental, brigade, division and army corps head-quarters were notified, and within ten minutes of the first sign of a movement, the entire position threatened was on the *qui vive* without excitement or confusion. But this was to be no ordinary attack; while preparations were still going forward, new symptoms never hitherto observed, were noticeable on the German line. Straw was thrown out beyond the trenches and was being sprinkled with a kind of white powder which the soldiers say resembled salt. While the Russians were still puzzling about the meaning of it all, fire was put to the straw in a dozen places. Instantly from the little spots of red flame spreading in both directions until the line of twinkling fire was continuous, huge clouds of fleecy white smoke rolled up. The officers were quick to realize what was coming, and instantly the word was passed to the soldiers that they must be prepared to meet a new kind of attack. After a rapid consultation and advice from head-quarters over the telephone, it was decided that it would be best for our men to remain absolutely quiet in their trenches, holding their fire until the enemy were at their barbed wire entanglements, in order to beguile the Germans into the belief that their gases were effective, and that they were going to be able to occupy the Russian trenches without losing a man.

Officers and non-commissioned officers went through the trenches telling the soldiers what they must expect, and imposing silence on all, and prohibiting the firing of a gun until the enemy were almost upon them when they were to open up with all the rapidity of fire that they could command. In the meantime the wind of early morning air was rolling the cloud gently toward the waiting Russians.

I have been able through certain channels, which I cannot at present mention, to secure a considerable amount of information as to the German side of this attack. When it became known in the trenches of the enemy that these gases were to be used, there is reason to believe that there was a protest from the soldiers against it. Many of the Russians are charitable enough to take the point of view that the common soldier resorts to these methods because he is forced to do so, and they say that the German private rebelled at the idea of using so hideous a method of conducting warfare. Others, while they accept the story of the soldiers' opposition, declare they only feared the effects of the gas upon themselves. In any event there is evidence that their officers told them that the gas was a harmless one, and would simply result in putting the Russians into a state of unconsciousness from which they would recover in a few hours, and by that time the Germans would have been able to take their trenches without the loss of a man. It was at first believed that the white powder placed on the straw was the element of the poison gas, but it later appeared that this was merely to produce a screen of heavy and harmless smoke behind which the real operations could be conducted. The actual source of the gas was in the trenches themselves.

Steel cylinders or tanks measuring a metre in length by perhaps 6 inches in width were let in end downwards into the floor of the trench, with perhaps half of the tanks firmly bedded in the ground. At the head of the cylinder was a valve, and from this ran a lead pipe over the top of the parapet and then bent downwards with the opening pointed to the ground. These tanks were arranged in groups of batteries the unit of which was ten or twelve, each tank being perhaps two feet from its neighbour. Between each group was a space of twenty paces. I have not been able to learn the exact length of the prepared trenches, but it was perhaps nearly a kilometre long. As soon as their line was masked by the volumes of the screening smoke, these taps were turned on simultaneously and instantly the thick greenish yellow fumes of the chloral gas poured in expanding clouds upon the ground, spreading like a mist upon the face of the earth.

There was a drift of air in the direction of the Russian trenches, and borne before this the poison rolled like a wave slowly away from the German line toward the positions of the Russians, the gas itself seeking out and filling each small hollow or declivity in the ground as surely as water, so heavy and thick was its composition. When it was fairly clear of their own line the Germans began to move, all the men having first been provided with respirators that they might not experience the effects of the "harmless and painless" gas prepared for the enemy. Ahead of the attacking columns went groups of sappers with shears to cut the Russian entanglements; and behind them followed the masses of the German infantry, while the rear was brought up, with characteristic foresight, by soldiers bearing tanks of oxygen to assist any of their own men who became unconscious from the fumes.

The advance started somewhat gingerly, for the soldiers do not seem to have had the same confidence in the effects of the gas as their officers. But as they moved forward there was not a sound from the Russian trench, and the word ran up and down the German line that there would be no defence, and that for once they would take a Russian position without the loss of a man. One can fancy the state of mind of the German troops in these few minutes. No doubt they felt that this new "painless" gas was going to be a humane way of ending the war, that their chemists had solved the great problem, and that in a few days they would be marching into Warsaw. Then they reached the Russian entanglements, and without warning were swept into heaps and mounds of collapsing bodies by the torrent of rifle and machine gun fire which came upon them from every loophole and cranny of the Russian position.

The Russian version of the story is one that must inspire the troops of the Allies, as it has inspired the rest of the army over here. Some time before the Germans actually approached, the green yellow cloud rolled into the trenches and poured itself in almost like a column of water; so heavy was it that it almost fell to the floor of the trenches. The patient Siberians stood without a tremor as it eddied around their feet and swept over their faces in constantly increasing volumes. Thus for some minutes they stood wrapping handkerchiefs about their faces, stifling their sounds, and uttering not a word while dozens fell suffocating into the trench. Then at last in the faint morning light could be seen the shadowy figures of the Germans through the mist; then at last discipline and self-control were released, and every soldier opened fire pumping out his cartridges from his rifle as fast as he could shoot. The stories of heroism and fortitude that one hears from the survivors of this trench are exceptional. One Siberian who was working a machine gun had asked his comrade to stand beside him with wet rags and a bucket of water. The two bodies were found together, the soldier collapsed over the machine gun, whose empty cartridge belt told the story of the man's last effort having gone to work his gun, while sprawling over the upset bucket was the dead body of the friend who had stood by and made his last task possible.

The colours of the Siberians.

Officers in the head-quarters of regiment and divisions tell of the operators at the telephones clinging to their instruments until only the sounds of their choking efforts to speak came over the wire, and then silence. Some were found dead with the receivers in their hands, while others were discovered clutching muskets fallen from the hands of the infantry that had succumbed. In this trying ordeal not a man, soldier or officer budged from his position. To a man they remained firm, some overcome, some dying, and others already dead. So faithful were they to their duty, that before the reserves reached them the Germans were already extricating themselves from their own dead and wounded, and hurriedly beating a retreat toward their own lines. From the rear trenches now came, leaping with hoarse shouts of fury, the columns of the Siberian reserves. Through the poisoned mist that curled and circled at their feet, they ran, many stumbling and falling from the effect of the noxious vapours. When they reached the first line trench, the enemy was already straggling back in retreat, a retreat that probably cost them more dearly than their attack; for the reserves, maddened with fury poured over their own trenches, pursued the Germans, and with clubbed rifle and bayonet took heavy vengeance for comrades poisoned and dying in the first line trench. So furiously did the Siberians fall upon the Germans that several positions in the German line were occupied, numbers of the enemy who chose to remain dying under the bayonet or else falling on their knees with prayers for mercy. Somewhat to the south of the main gas attack there came a change in the wind, and the poisoned fumes blew back into the trenches of the Germans, trenches in which it is believed the occupants were not equipped with respirators. The Russians in opposite lines say that the cries of the Germans attacked by their own fumes were something horrible to listen to, and their shrieks could have been heard half a mile away.

Thus ended the first German effort to turn the Russians out of their positions by the use of a method which their rulers had pledged themselves in treaty never to adopt. The net results were an absolute defeat of the Germans, with the loss of several of their own positions, and a loss in dead and wounded probably three times greater than was suffered by the Russians. Even although it was unexpected and unprepared for, this first attempt was an absolute failure; the only result being an increase of fury on the part of the Russian soldiers that makes it difficult to keep them in their trenches, so eager are they to go over and bayonet their enemies.

CHAPTER XII
SOME DETAILS REGARDING THE GAS HORROR

WARSAW,
June 8.

EVER since my return from the southern armies last week I have spent practically my entire time in the study and investigation of the newest phase of frightfulness as practised by the German authorities. Ten months of war and an earlier experience in Manchuria of what misery it represents even when conducted in the most humane way have not tended to make me over-sensitive to the sights and sufferings which are the inevitable accompaniment of the conflict between modern armies; but what I have seen in the last week has impressed me more deeply than the sum total of all the other horrors which I have seen in this and other campaigns combined. The effects of the new war methods involve hideous suffering and are of no military value whatsoever (if results on this front are typical); while they reduce war to a barbarity and cruelty which could not be justified from any point of view, even were the results obtained for the cause of the user a thousandfold greater than they have proved to be.

I found on my return from the south the whole of Warsaw in a fever of riotous indignation against the Germans and the German people as the result of the arrival of the first block of gas victims brought in from the Bzura front. I have already described the attack made on the Russian position, its absolute failure, and the result it had of increasing the morale of the Russian troops. I must now try to convey to the reader an idea of the effects which I have personally witnessed and ascertained by first hand investigation of the whole subject. The investigation has taken me from the Warsaw hospitals, down through the various army, corps, division and regimental head-quarters, to the advance trenches on which the attack was actually made. I have talked with every one possible, from generals to privates, and from surgeons to the nurses, and to the victims themselves, and feel, therefore, that I can write with a fair degree of authority.

The gas itself, I was told at the front, was almost pure chloral fumes; but in the hospitals here they informed me that there were indications of the presence of a small trace of bromine, though it has proved somewhat difficult to make an exact analysis. The effect of the gas when inhaled is to cause an immediate and extremely painful irritation of the lungs and the bronchial tubes, which causes instantly acute suffering. The gas, on reaching the lungs, and coming in contact with the blood, at once causes congestion, and clots begin to form not only in the lungs themselves but in the blood-vessels and larger arteries, while the blood itself becomes so thick that it is with great difficulty that the heart is able to force it through the veins. The first effects, then, are those of strangulation, pains throughout the body where clots are forming, and the additional misery of the irritation which the acid gases cause to all the mucous membranes to which it is exposed. Some of the fatal cases were examined by the surgeons on the post-mortem table, and it was found that the lungs were so choked with coagulated blood that, as one doctor at the front told me, they resembled huge slabs of raw liver rather than lungs at all. The heart was badly strained from the endeavour to exert its functions against such obstacles, and death had resulted from strangulation.

Though the unfortunates who succumbed suffered hideously, their lot was an easy one compared to the lot of the miserable wretches who lingered on and died later. One might almost say that even those that are recovering have suffered so excruciatingly as to make life dear at the price. Those who could be treated promptly have for the most part struggled back to life. Time only will show whether they recover entirely, but from evidence obtained, I am inclined to believe many of them will be restored to a moderate condition of good health after their lungs are healed. The first treatment employed by the Russians when their patients come to the hospitals, is to strip them of all clothing, give them a hot bath and put them into clean garments. This is done for the protection of the nurses as well as of the victims, for it was found that many of the helpers were overcome by the residue of the fumes left in the clothing, so deadly was the nature of the chemical compound used.

Even after these cases were brought to Warsaw and put into clean linen pyjamas and immaculate beds, the gas still given out from their lungs as they exhaled so poisoned the air in the hospital that some of the women nurses were affected with severe headaches and with nausea. From this it may be gathered that the potency of the chloral compound is extremely deadly. The incredible part is, that out of the thousands affected, hardly a thousand died in the trenches, and of the 1,300 to 1,500 brought to Warsaw, only 2 per cent. have died to date. It is probably true that the Russian moujik soldier is the hardiest individual in Europe; add to this the consideration that for ten months none of them have been touching alcohol, which is probably one reason for their astonishing vitality in fighting this deadly poison and struggling back to life.

Respirator drill in the trenches.

Austrians leaving Przemysl.

After the victims are washed, every effort is made to relieve the congestion. Mustard plasters are applied to the feet, while camphor injections are given hypodermically, and caffeine or, in desperate cases, digitalis is given to help the heart keep up its task against the heavy odds. Next blood is drawn from the patient and quantities of salt and water injected in the veins to take its place and to dilute what remains. In the severer cases I am told that the blood even from the arteries barely flows, and comes out a deep purple and almost as viscous as molasses. In the far-gone cases it refuses to flow at all.

The victims that die quickly are spared the worst effects, but those that linger on and finally succumb suffer a torture which the days of the Inquisition can hardly parallel. Many of them have in their efforts to breathe swallowed quantities of the gas, and in these cases, which seem to be common, post-mortems disclose the fact that great patches in their stomachs and in their intestines have been eaten almost raw by the action of the acid in the gas. These men then die not only of strangulation, which, in itself, is a slow torture, but in their last moments their internal organs are slowly being eaten away by the acids which they have taken into their stomachs. Several of the doctors have told me that in these instances the men go violently mad from sheer agony, and that many of them must be held in their beds by force to prevent them from leaping out of the windows or running amok in the hospitals. It is hard to still them with sufficient morphine to deaden the pain without giving an overdose, with the result that many of the poor fellows probably suffer until their last gasp.

This then is the physical effect which is produced on the victims of Germany's latest device to win the war. I have been in many of the hospitals, and I have never in my life been more deeply moved than by the pathetic spectacle of these magnificent specimens of manhood lying on their beds writhing in pain or gasping for breath, each struggle being a torture. The Russians endure suffering with a stoicism that is heartbreaking to observe, and I think it would surely touch even the most cynical German chemist were he to see his victims, purple in the face, lips frothed with red from bleeding lungs, with head thrown back and teeth clenched to keep back the groans of anguish, as they struggle against the subtle poison that has been taken into their system. One poor fellow said to the nurse as she sat by his bed and held his hand, "Oh, if the German Kaiser could but suffer the pain that I do he would never inflict this torture upon us. Surely there must be a horrible place prepared for him in the hereafter."

The effect upon the troops at the front who have seen the sufferings of their fellows or who have had a touch of it themselves, has been quite extraordinary. Some of the more cynical say that the German idea involved this suffering as a part of their campaign of frightfulness, their belief being that it would strike panic to the hearts of all the soldiers that beheld it and result in the utter demoralization of the Russian Army. If this be true the German psychologists never made a more stupid blunder, for in this single night's work they have built up for themselves in the heart of every Russian moujik a personal hatred and detestation that has spread like wildfire in all parts of the army and has made the Russian troops infinitely fiercer both in attack and in defence than at any other period in the war. Not a soldier or officer with whom I have talked has shown the smallest sign of fear for the future, and all are praying for an opportunity to exact a vengeance.

Unfortunately in the next attacks in which this just fury will be in evidence, it will be the unfortunate German soldier who must pay the price at the point of the bayonet, while the cold-blooded wretches who worked it all out will go scot free from the retribution which the Russians intend to administer with cold steel and the butt end of their muskets. In the meantime the Russians have taken steps which will in all probability render future attacks practically innocuous. Every soldier is receiving a respirator, a small mask soaked in some chemical preparation and done up in an air-tight packet ready for use. The preparation, it is believed, will keep out the fumes for at least an hour. It is highly improbable that any such period will elapse before the gases are dissipated by the wind; but in any event extra quantities of the solution will be kept in the trenches to enable the soldiers to freshen their masks if the gases are not cleared up within an hour.

In addition to this, open ditches will be dug in the trenches and filled with water, which will promptly suck up the gas that would otherwise linger on indefinitely. It is also proposed to strew straw in front of the positions and to sprinkle it with water before an attack with the gases in order to take up as much of the poison as possible before it reaches the trenches at all. When one remembers that though the first attack came without any preparations being made to meet it, and was an absolutely new experience to the Russians, it yet failed overwhelmingly, I think one need feel no anxiety as to the results which will follow the next attack when every preparation has been made by the Russians to receive it.

I have dwelt at some length on the subject of the poisoned gases, but as there is available evidence to indicate that the Germans are planning to make this an important feature of their campaign, it seems worth while to bring before the attention of the outside world all of the consequences which the use of this practice involve. I hear now from excellent sources that the Germans are equipping a large plant at Plonsk for the express purpose of making poison gases on a large scale. In what I have written before I have only mentioned the bearing of the gas on strictly military operations, but there is another consideration to be noticed in this new practice, and that is the effect which it has, and will have increasingly, upon the unfortunate peasant and civil population whose miserable fate it is to live behind the lines.

I am not aware of the nature and potency of the gas used in the West, but I read recently in the paper that it was so deadly that its effects were observable a full mile from the line of battle. Over here they were noticeable 25 miles from the line, and individuals were overcome as far away as 14 versts from the positions. The General commanding the — Siberian Corps told me that the sentry before his gate fell to the ground from inhaling the poisoned air, though his head-quarters is more than 10 miles away from the point where the Germans turned loose their fiendish invention. The General commanding the —th Division of this same Siberian Corps, against whom the attack was made, told me that the gases reached his head-quarters exactly 1½ hours after it passed the positions which he told me were between 5 and 6 versts from the house in which he lived. In the morning the fumes lay like a mist on the grass, and later in the day they were felt with sufficient potency to cause nausea and headaches at Grodisk, 30 versts from the trenches. Everywhere I was told of the suffering and panic among the peasants, who came staggering in from every direction to the Russian Red Cross stations and head-quarters. These, of course, were not as severely stricken as the troops in the front lines, and as far as I know none of them have died, but hundreds were being cared for by the Russian authorities, and among these I am told were many women and children.

Siberians returning from the trenches.

In fact it is but logical to expect the greatest suffering in the future to be among children, for the gas hangs very low, and where a six foot man might keep his nose clear of the fumes, a child of two or three years old would be almost sure to perish. The live stock suffered more or less, but there seems to have been a great difference in the effects of the gases upon different kinds of animals. Horses were driven almost frantic, cows felt it much less, and pigs are said not to have been bothered appreciably. In its effects on plants and flowers one notices a great range of results among different varieties. Pansies were slightly wilted, snapdragons absolutely, while certain little blue flowers whose name I do not know were scarcely affected at all. Some of the tips of the grasses were coloured brown, while leaves on some trees were completely destitute of any colour at all. I cannot explain the varying effects. I have in my pocket a leaf two-thirds of which is as white as a piece of writing paper while the remaining third is as green as grass. On the same tree some leaves were killed and others not affected at all. The effects also vary greatly in different parts of the country. From what I could observe the gas had flowed to all the low places where it hung for hours. In the woods it is said to have drifted about with bad effects that lasted for several days.

What I have described above is the first effect on the country, but if the Germans are to continue this practice for the rest of the summer I think there must be effects which in the end will result in far more injury to the peasants who are not prepared, than to the soldiers who are taught how to combat the gases. In the first place it seems extremely probable that this gas flowing to the low places will almost invariably settle in the lakes, marshes and all bodies of still water within 20 to 30 versts of the line. I am not sufficiently well grounded in chemistry to speak authoritatively, but it seems not improbable that the effect of this will be gradually to transform every small body of water in this vicinity into a diluted solution of hydrochloric acid, a solution which will become more and more concentrated with every wave of gas that passes over the country-side. If this be the case Poland may perhaps see huge numbers of its horses, cows and other live stock slowly poisoned by chloral while the inhabitants may experience a similar fate. With wet weather and moist soil will come a period when the chloral will go into the earth in large quantities. I do not know what effect this will have on the future of the crops, but I imagine that it will not help the harvest this year, while its deleterious effects may extend over many to come. In other words it seems as though the Germans in order to inflict a possible military damage on the Russians are planning a campaign, the terrible effects of which will fall for the most part not on the soldiers at all but on the harmless non-combatants who live in the rear of the lines. This practice is as absolutely unjustifiable as that of setting floating mines loose at sea on the possible chance of sinking an enemy ship, the probability being ten to one that the victim will prove an innocent one.

We are now facing over here, and I suppose in the West as well, a campaign of poisoned air, the effect of which upon the military situation will be neutralized by reprisals; but at the same time this campaign is going to increase the suffering and misery of the soldiers a hundred per cent., and in its ultimate results bring more misery to the populations in the various regions near the lines than has ever been experienced in any previous war. It must be reasonably clear to the Germans by now that their scheme to terrorize has failed, and that their aim of inflicting vast damage has fallen to the ground. When reprisals come, as they must if Germany continues this inhuman policy, she will, without having gained anything whatsoever from her experiment, cause needlessly the deaths of thousands of her own soldiers, as well as suffering and devastation among the rural classes. It does seem as though, when the German policy is so clearly unfruitful, it should be possible through the medium of some neutral country to reach an agreement providing for the entire discontinuance on all fronts of this horrible practice. Certainly, when there are so many thousands of innocents who must suffer by its continuance, it would be well worth the while of the authorities in the different countries to consider the possibility mentioned before resorting to the use of this deadly weapon, which often proves as dangerous to the users as to the enemy against whom it is directed.

CHAPTER XIII
THE BZURA FRONT IN JUNE

Dated:
WARSAW,
June 9.

SOME one has said that there is nothing more monotonous than war. After ten months of almost continuous contact with its various phenomena, and week after week spent in the same atmosphere, where one is always surrounded by the same types of men in the same uniforms, the same transport, the same guns, the same Red Cross, and in fact everything the same in general appearance, it becomes very difficult to get up new interest in the surroundings, and that deadly monotony of even the happenings makes it increasingly difficult to write about it. The types of country vary here and trenches are not after one pattern, but after one has seen a few dozen even of these there is a good deal of sameness in it all. I have not been on the Bzura Front, however, since January, and as little has been written about it by any one else since the big January-February attacks on the Bolimov positions, it may be worth devoting a short chapter to it, describing its appearance in summer.

The last time that I was out here was in January, when the ground was deep in snow and slush, and the soldiers muffled to their ears to keep out the biting winds that swept across the country. Now the whole army, that is not fighting or otherwise occupied, is luxuriously basking in the sunshine, or idling under the shade of the trees. The poisonous gas campaigns, of which I have already written at length, having been started on our Bzura line, seemed to justify a visit to the positions here in order that I might speak with some degree of accuracy as to the effects of this newest German method of warfare, from the trenches, where the attacks were made, down through the varying stages to the last, where one found the victims struggling for breath in the Warsaw hospitals.

Leaving Warsaw early in the morning I went to the head-quarters of the army immediately before Warsaw, and on explaining my desires, every possible means of assistance was placed at my disposal including an extra automobile and an officer interpreter. From the army head-quarters we sped over a newly-built road to the head-quarters of that army corps which is defending the line of the Rawka, where the chief medical officer obligingly placed at my disposal all the information which he possessed of the General commanding that particular Siberian army corps on whom the experiment was first tried. This man, an officer of high rank, was living in a small white cottage standing by the side of a second rate country road, without a single tree to protect it from the rays of the sun which in the afternoon was beating down on it with a heat that could be seen as it shimmered up from the baking earth, barren of grass or any green thing. Here was a man, commanding perhaps 40,000 troops, living in one of the bleakest spots I have seen in Poland, with nothing but a tiny head-quarters flag and dozens of telephone wires running in from all directions to denote that he was directing a command greater than a battalion.

As the greatest indignation prevails throughout the army on the gas subject, I found the officers here very eager to help me in my investigations, and the General immediately telephoned to the division head-quarters that we would visit them and asked that an officer might be provided to take us forward to the positions where the heaviest losses occurred. So once more we took to our motor car, and for another 6 versts, across fields and down avenues of trees, we sped until at last we turned off sharply into the country estate of some landed proprietor where were living the staff of the —th division. These fortunate men were much better off than their commander, for in a lovely villa, with a lake shimmering like a sheet of silver in the sunlight behind the terrace on which the officers could have their coffee in the evenings, the General and his suite lived. A delightful little Captain, who seemed to be in charge of our programme, led us to a window and pointing to a windmill in an adjacent field remarked: "The German artillery reaches just to that point. From the time you leave there until you reach the trenches you will be continually within the range of their guns and for most of the time within plain sight of their observers in their gun positions. However, if you insist we shall be glad to let you go. Probably they will not fire on you, and if they do I think they will not hit you. An automobile is a difficult target."

With this doubtful assurance we started out again, this time heading for regimental head-quarters, which we were told was a mile behind the trenches. A few miles further, and we came on several battalions in reserve near a little village. A small orchard here gave them shelter from observation, and after their trying ordeal a few days before, they were resting luxuriously on the grass, many of them lying flat on their backs in the shade fast asleep while everywhere were piled their rifles. These sturdy self-respecting Siberian troops are the cream of the army and physically as fine specimens of manhood as I have ever seen anywhere. From this point we turned sharply west and ran at top speed down an avenue of trees to a little bridge, where we left the car effectively concealed behind a clump of trees. At least that was the intention, and one in which the chauffeur and his orderly companion took great interest as one could see by the careful scrutiny that they gave the landscape and then their cover.

Personally I think this is the meanest country to get about in during the day time that I can possibly imagine. It is almost as flat as a billiard table, and I am of the opinion that if you lay down in the road you could see a black pin sticking up in it a mile away. Everything around you is as still as death for perhaps ten minutes. The sun shines, butterflies flit about and an occasional bee goes droning past. There is nothing whatever to suggest the possibility of war. You think it is a mistake and that you are at least twenty miles from the Front; then you hear a deep detonation not far away and a great smoking crater in a field near by indicates where a heavy shell has burst. Again there is absolute silence for perhaps twenty minutes, when a sharp report not far away causes you to look quickly toward a grove of trees in a neighbouring field where you discover one of the Russian batteries. Leaving our motor we walk across a field and approach the site of a destroyed village, if a cluster of six or eight little cottages could ever have been dignified by that name. Now only a chimney here, or a few walls there, indicates where once stood this little group of homes. In one of the ruins, like a dog in an ash-heap, lives the Colonel of the —th Siberian with his staff. Behind a wall left standing is a table and a few chairs, and dug out of the corner is a bomb proof where converge telephones from the trenches in which are his troops. Here he has been living since the middle of last January.

The village was destroyed months and months ago, and clearly as it is in the line of German observation it seems to provide a comparatively safe retreat for the officers, though as one of them remarked quite casually, "They dropped thirty-five shells round us yesterday, but you see nothing much came of it." Absolute indifference to these situations is the keynote at the Front, and good form makes one refrain from asking the numerous questions as to the exact location of the enemy, whether or not they can see us, and other subjects which, at the moment, seem to us of first-class importance. However, we realize that good taste requires that we assume the same casual attitude, and so we sit for half an hour, smoke cigarettes and quietly hope that the enemy will choose some other target than this for their afternoon practice which, as one of the officers remarked, "Usually begins about this hour in the afternoon."

Personally I hate poking around in the broad daylight in this flat country, but as I wanted to see the position where the gas was used and did not want to wait until night, and as the Colonel was perfectly agreeable, I suggested that we should proceed forthwith to the positions. Before starting we were told that up to a few weeks ago no one ever used the road in the daytime, because of its exposure to rifle and artillery fire. "But now," as the Colonel said, "for some reason or other they are not shooting at individuals. Probably they are saving their ammunition for Galicia. So if we walk apart we shall not be in much danger. Anyway a man or two would be hard to hit with rifle fire, and their artillery is rather poor here, and even if they fire at us I think we shall not be killed." We thanked him for his optimism and all started off down the road that led to the positions. In view of his suggestion about individuals being safe, I was not particularly happy when five officers who had nothing else to do joined us. The first half mile of the road led down an avenue of trees which effectively screened us. After that the trees stopped and the great white road, elevated about 5 feet above the surrounding country, impressed me as being the most conspicuous topographical feature that I had seen in Poland. There was not a bit of brush as big as a tooth-pick to conceal our party walking serenely down the highway.

After we had got about 200 yards on this causeway the Colonel stopped and pointed with his stick at a group of red brick buildings. "The Germans were there," translated the interpreter. "My," I ejaculated in enthusiasm at the idea that they had gone, "when did we retake the position?" "Oh," replied the interpreter officer, "not yet. They are still there." "Ah!" I said, lighting a cigarette, that my interest might not seem too acute, "I should think they could see us." The linguist spoke a few words to the Colonel and then replied, "Oh, yes, every move we make, but the Colonel thinks they will not shoot." I looked over at the brick buildings, behind which were the German artillery positions, and I could swear they were not 2,000 yards away, while a line of dirt nearer still showed the infantry trenches. For myself I felt as large as an elephant, and to my eyes our party seemed as conspicuous as Barnum's circus on parade. However we continued our afternoon stroll to the reserve trenches, where a soldier or two joined our group. Five or six hundred yards up the road was the barricade thrown across, held by the first line. An occasional crack of a rifle reminded us that the look-outs in our trenches were studying the movements in the German trenches a few hundred yards beyond. Finally we left the road and came over a field and into the rear of our own position, and to the scene of the German gas attacks four or five days before.

Life in the trenches has become such an everyday affair to these sunburned, brawny soldiers from Siberia that they seem to have no more feeling of anxiety than if they were living in their own villages far, far to the East. In spite of the fact that they have steadily borne the brunt of terrible attacks, and even now are under the shadow of the opposing lines, which are thoroughly equipped with the mechanism for dispensing poisoned air, they are as gay and cheerful as schoolboys on a vacation. I have never seen such healthy, high-spirited soldiers in my life. The trenches have been so cleaned up that a house wife could find no fault with them.

These homes of the soldiers have every appearance of being swept daily. The apprehension felt in the winter of hygienic conditions when the spring came have no ground whatever, and I am told on the very highest authority that in this army the sickness, other than that coming from wounds, is less than for the months that preceded the war itself. The Colonel explained to us the use of the respirators with which every soldier is provided, and for our benefit had one of the soldiers fitted with one that he might be photographed to illustrate for the West what sort of protection is being supplied to the men on this side. After spending half to three-quarters of an hour wandering about in the trenches and meeting the officers who live there we returned to the regimental head-quarters. The sun was just setting, and as we strolled back over the open causeway in its last red glow a great German battery suddenly came into action somewhere off to the west and north of us, and we could hear the heavy detonations of its huge shells falling in a nearby wood.

When we got back to the regimental head-quarters I could see their target, which seemed to be nothing more than a big field. Every few minutes an enormous shell would drop in the meadow. For an instant there would be but a little dust where it hit the ground, then suddenly a great spout of earth and dust and volumes of dirty brown smoke would leap into the air like the eruption of a volcano, and then the heavy sound of the explosion would reach our ears, while for two or three minutes the crater would smoke as though the earth itself were being consumed by hidden fires. As it was coming late we did not linger long at the head-quarters but took to our car and sped up the avenue of trees which lay directly parallel to the point where the shells were bursting. The sun had set now, and in the after glow we passed once more the camps of the reserves squatting about their little twinkling fires built in the earth to mask them from the sight of the enemy. In half an hour we were back once more in the villa of the General of the division, an enormous man of six feet three, whose cross of St. George of the first class was given for a heroic record in Manchuria where the General, then a Colonel, was three times wounded by Japanese bullets. Sitting on his terrace he gave us more details in regard to the usages of the gas against his troops. Though they were 6 versts from the Front, everyone in his head-quarters had been affected with nausea and headaches, so potent were the fumes of the chloral that for hours lay like a miasmic mist in the grounds and garden of the estate. The General, who is a very kindly giant, shook his head sadly as he spoke of the Germans. I think the Russians are a very charitable people and nearly all the men with whom I have talked lay the blame of this outrage on civilization against the authorities and not against the men, who, they understand, are bitterly opposed to its use. When I asked the General what he thought of the German point of view of war, he sat for a few moments looking out over the lovely garden with the little lake that lay before us.

"They have an extraordinary point of view," he said at last. Then he rose quickly from his chair and brought from a corner of the balcony a belt captured in some skirmish of the morning. He held it up for me to see the big buckle and with his finger pointed to the words: "GOTT MIT UNS." Then with a smile more significant than words he tossed it back into the corner. Yes, truly, the German point of view is an extraordinary one.

CHAPTER XIV
THE GALICIAN FRONT

Dated:
ROVNA,
June 26, 1915.

IN a few weeks a year will have passed since the Imperial German Government began issuing its series of declarations of war against one country after another—declarations which as time elapses are assuming the aspect of hostilities not only against individual countries, but against practically all that modern civilization had come to represent. During that time each of the Allies, and all of the world besides, have been studying the geography of Europe and the armies engaged in the great conflict. Of all these countries and of all these armies, I think that the least known and the least understood are the country and the army of Russia.

It has been my fortune to be with the Russians since last September, during which time I have travelled thousands of versts both in Poland and in Galicia. I have visited eight out of their eleven active armies, and been on the positions in most of them, and it is not an exaggeration to say that I have met and talked with between five hundred and a thousand officers. Yet I feel that I am only now beginning to realize what this war means to Russia, and the temper that it has slowly but surely developed in her armies and in her peoples. Never I think have the stamina and the temper of a country been more fiercely tested than have those of Russia during the campaign which has been going on in Galicia since May last. All the world realizes in a general way what the Russians had to contend with, and all the world knows vaguely that Russia has a front of 1,200 versts to protect, and appreciates in an indefinite kind of way that such a line must be difficult to hold. But though I have been here for eleven months, I never formed any adequate conception of how great was this problem until I undertook to cover the Front, from its far fringe in Bukovina to its centre on the Warsaw Front.

During the past two months it has been all but impossible to follow movements with any clear understanding of their significance. We have all known that the Russians were retiring from position after position before overwhelming attacks of the enemy; and with very few exceptions, the world has concluded, and the enemy certainly has, that flying before the phalanx of the Austro-German legions with their thousands of massed guns, fed with clockwork regularity with munitions and supplies brought up by their superb railway systems, was the wrecked and defeated Russian Army, an organization that it would take months of rest and recuperation to lick into the shape of a virile fighting force once more. I have never shared this opinion myself, for we who were in Manchuria ten years ago learned to know that though it was quite possible to drive the Russians off the field, it was equally impossible to destroy their *moral* or break their spirits. A month after Lio Yang the supposedly defeated Russians took the offensive at Sha Ho and came a cropper. Again in January another offensive was developed and failed. They were ready once more at Moukden and lost badly. By September had peace not intervened they would have fought again. Even the Japanese were beginning to feel the discouragement of the Russian persistency in refusing to accept defeat as final. The Manchurian campaign was unpopular, not in the least understood, and yet the Russian moujik hung on and on month after month. The Japanese knew their mettle and admitted it freely.

For a year now we have had the Russians again at war. But this time the situation is quite different. The war touched the slow lethargic rather negative Russian temperament from the start, by its appeal to their race sympathies, which is the one vital chord that can always be touched with a certainty of response, in the heart of every Slav. From the first month, the popularity of the war has grown steadily, until to-day it has the backing of the entire Russian people, barring isolated groups of intriguers and cliques controlled and influenced by German blood. I have talked with officers from every part of this Empire, and they all tell me that it is the same in Siberia as it is in European Russia. The moujik in his heavy, ponderous way is behind this war. No matter what pessimism one hears in Petrograd or Warsaw, one can always find consolation as to the ultimate outcome by going to the common people, those who patiently and stoically are bearing the burden. This is the strength of Russia and this is why Russia and the Russian Armies are not beaten in Galicia, are not discouraged and have not the vaguest idea of a peace without a decision any more than the Englishman, the Frenchman or the Belgian.

In so vast a theatre as this, it is utterly impossible to form clear and definite opinions as to what has taken place even in the past year, and it may be imagined with what difficulty one can predict the future. But there is one thing in war that is greater than an advance or a retreat, greater than a dozen battles, and greater than the speculations of experts, and that thing is the temper and stamina of the men and the people who are fighting the war. Given that and one can look with comparative equanimity upon the ups and downs of the vast tactical and strategical problems which develop now in East Prussia, now in Poland and again in Galicia. There was one great strategic aim of the Germans in their Galician movement, and that was to crush the Russian Army, hand back to Austria her lost province, and then hurry back to the west to attack England and France. It is true that Germany has driven the Russians from position after position; it is true that she has given back Lwow to the unenthusiastic Austrians, who with trembling hands accepted it back as a dangerous gift, and it is true that the world looks upon the recapture of Galicia as a great moral blow to the Russian arms. Thus far has Germany achieved her ends. But she has not destroyed the army, she has not discouraged the troops, and with the exception of one army, now repaired, she did not even seriously cripple it.

The plain facts are, that by a preponderance of war munitions which Russia could not equal, supplied over lines of communication which Russia could not duplicate, Germany forced Russian withdrawals before her, for men cannot fight modern battles with their fists. The glory of the German advance will be dimmed when the world really knows exactly what Russia had in men and in arms and munitions to meet this assault, the greatest perhaps that has ever been made in military history. Indeed the surprise of the writer is not that the Germans won but that they did not crush the army before them. This retreat from the Dunajec will form a brilliant page in Russia's history, and an object lesson to the whole world of what a stubborn army composed of courageous hearts can do by almost sheer bravery alone. The Russians have come through their trial by fire. Barring one army they have probably suffered far less in personnel than the loss they have inflicted on their enemy. They have reached, or approximately reached, another point of defence. Their spirits are good, their confidence unshaken, and their determination to fight on indefinitely, regardless of defeats, is greater than it ever was before.

The Germans have failed in their greatest aim—as the case stands to-day. One cannot doubt that the high authorities in Berlin must realize this truth as surely as the military brains do on this side of the line. The Germans have shot their first bolt, a bolt forged from every resource in men and munitions that they could muster after months of preparation. The Russians have recoiled before it and may recoil again and again, but they always manage to prevent it from accomplishing its aim. At the moment of writing Germany faces the identical problem that she did two months ago, excepting that she now occupies extra territory, for the most part in ruins. The problem before her is to repeat the Galician enterprise on an army infinitely better than the one she broke in May. If she can do this she will have the identical problem to meet on some other line in another two months, and after that another and another. It is simply a question of how much time, men and resources Germany has to spend on these costly victories, if indeed the next proves a victory, which is doubtful. She may do it once, she may do it twice, but whenever it may be there will come a time when she can do it no more, and when that time comes Russia will slowly, surely, inexorably come back, step by step, until she has regained her own, her early conquests, and has Germany on her knees in the East. It is futile to speculate as to time. It may be months and it may be years. But it is most surely coming eventually.

CHAPTER XV
THE GERMAN DRIVE IN GALICIA

Dated:
ROVNA,
June 26, 1915.

IT is utterly impossible at this time to give anything like an accurate story of the past two months in Galicia. It will be years before the information necessary for definite history can be accumulated from the various units engaged. Even then there will be gaps and inaccuracies because hundreds of the men engaged have been killed, and so few even of the Generals know more than their own side of the case, that the difficulties of the historian will be enormous.

I shall not attempt then, in this brief chapter, anything but to trace the merest outline of the causes and effects of the German drive in Galicia.

It has been apparent to all of us here from the start of the war that Warsaw was becoming increasingly the German objective. Attempts from the north and on the centre failed absolutely, the latter both in October and in January-February, and the former in September and in March. The fall of Przemysl and the Russian advance in the Carpathians, with the even greater menace to the Hungarian plain by the army operating in Bukovina, was threatening Austria with absolute collapse. The extreme eastern army with its drives further and further toward Hungary is said to have brought Hungary to the verge of openly demanding a separate peace. All these causes, then, rendered it necessary for Germany to do something for Austria, and by clearing out Galicia she hoped, not only to restore to her broken ally something of hope and spirit, but no doubt conceived the belief that by the time she had done this, she would be sufficiently far east and south of Warsaw to threaten it from the south and rear, and possibly cause its abandonment without a real battle near Warsaw at all. Many people here believe that the Germans want merely to secure and hold the line of the Vistula and Galicia, and then concentrate all their attention on the west. After the echoes of the fighting north of Warsaw in February-March were dying away, it became clear to all of us here that there would soon be another blow in some other quarter. Russia, as one so often repeats, has this enormous line. She cannot be in strength at every point, and though she saw for several weeks that the Germans were concentrating on the Dunajec line in Galicia, she could not reinforce it sufficiently to hold it without weakening other more vital points. As a fact, under the conditions which actually developed there she could not have held it, nor I think could any other army.

The world's history records nothing that has even approximated to this German drive which fell on one Russian Army, the bulk of which remained at its post and perished. The total number of German army corps sent down to do this job is uncertain. I have heard from many in high authority estimates differing so widely that I can supply no statement as absolutely correct. Perhaps sixteen is not far from the actual number, though probably reinforcements and extra divisions sent in pretty steadily to fill losses, brought up the total to a larger number than the full strength of sixteen corps. However the details at this time are immaterial. The main point is that the Russians were entirely outnumbered in men, guns and ammunition. The statements about the German massed guns also vary as widely as from 2,000 to 4,000. Certainly they had not less than 200 guns equal to or exceeding 8-inch types. These were concentrated on the front which was held by three or four corps of the devoted Dunajec army.

Men who know have told me that what followed was indescribable. I have not heard that there was any panic, or attempt to retreat on the part of the troops. In characteristic Russian fashion they remained and took their gruelling. For whole versts behind the line, I am told that the terrain was a hash of earth, mangled bodies, and fragments of exploded shell. If the statement that the Germans fired 700,000 shells in three hours is true, and it is accepted in the Russian Army, one can readily realize what must have been the condition of the army occupying that line of works. Much criticism has been brought against the General commanding because he had no well-prepared second line of trenches. No doubt he ought to have had it, but it would have made little difference beyond delaying the advance a few days. The German machine had been preparing for two months, and everything was running as smooth as a well-oiled engine, with troops, munitions and supplies being fed in with precision and regularity.

Russia is not an industrial nation, and cannot turn her resources into war material overnight as the Germans have been able to do. She was outclassed in everything except bravery, and neither the Germans nor any other army can claim superiority to her in that respect. With the centre literally cut away, the keystone of the Russian line had been pulled out, and nothing remained but to retire. In this retirement five Russian Armies were involved. Beginning on the right was that of Evert lying entirely in Poland on the Nida river. His army has been usually successful and always full of fight, and its retirement was purely that it might keep symmetrical with the Russian line as a whole. I have written in an earlier chapter of Evert's retreat, of how in falling back on to his new line he accounted for between 20,000 and 30,000 of the German and Austrian troops. Of this it is unnecessary to say more at present, save that his army is in a good position and stronger and more spirited than ever.

General Brussilov.

The unfortunate army of the Dunajec, whose commander and number are as well known in England as here, began then to fall back with what there was left of it on the San, tearing up railroads and fighting a rearguard action with what strength it could command. In the meantime the army of Brussilov, which up to this time had never been defeated, was well through the Carpathians and going strong. The crumbling of their right neighbour left them in a terrible plight, and only skilful and rapid manœuvring got them back out of the passes in time to get in touch with the fragments of the retreating centre, which by the time it reached the San had got reinforcements and some ammunition. Brussilov's right tried to hold Przemysl, but as the commander assured me, there was nothing left of the fortifications. Besides, as I gather from officers in that part of his army, further retirements of the next army kept exposing their flank, and made it imperative for the whole army to commence its retreat toward the Russian frontier.

I have good reason for believing that the Russian plan to retire to their own frontier was decided on when they lost Przemysl, and that the battles on the Grodek line, around Lwow, were merely rearguard actions. In any case, I do know that while the fighting was still in progress on the San, and just as Przemysl was taken, work was commenced on a permanent line of defence south of Lublin and Cholm, the line in fact which is at this moment being held by the Russians. My belief, then, is that everything that took place between the San and the present line must be considered inevitable in the higher interests of Russian strategy. The interim between leaving the San and taking up what is now approximately the line on which they will probably make a definite stand, will make a very fine page in Russian history. I cannot at this time go into any details, but the Allies will open their eyes when they know exactly how little the Russians had in the way of ammunition to hold off this mass of Germans and Austrians whose supply of shell poured in steadily week after week.

Next to the army of Brussilov is that army which had been assaulting and making excellent headway in the Eastern Carpathians. They, too, were attacked with terrible energy, but taken independently could probably have held on indefinitely. As it was they never moved until the retirement of all the other armies west of them rendered their position untenable. The German and Austrian communiques have constantly discussed the defeat of this army. The world can judge whether it was demoralized when it learns that in six weeks, from Stryj to the Zota Lipa, it captured 53,000 prisoners. During this same period, the army of Bukovina in the far left was actually advancing, and only came back to preserve the symmetry of the whole line. The problem of falling back over this extremely long front with five great armies, after the centre was completely broken, was as difficult an one as could well be presented. In the face of an alert enemy there were here and there local disasters and bags of Russian prisoners, but with all their skill, and with all their railroads, and superiority in both men and ammunition, the Germans and the Austrians have not been able to destroy the Russian force, which stands before them to-day on a new and stronger line. The further the Russians have retired, the slower has been their retreat and the more difficult has it been for the enemy to follow up their strokes with anything like the same strength and energy. In other words the Russians are pretty nearly beyond the reach of enemy blows which can hurt them fatally.

The Austrians have followed up the Eastern armies and claim enormous victories, but it must be pretty clear now, even to the Austrians and Germans, that these victories, which are costing them twice what they are costing the Russians, are merely rearguard actions. In any case the Austrian enthusiasm is rapidly ebbing away. After two months of fighting the Germans have finally swung their main strength back toward the line of Cholm-Lublin, with the probable intent of finishing up the movement by threatening Warsaw and thus closing up successfully the whole Galician campaign, which as many believe, had this end in view. But now they find a recuperated and much stronger Russian Army complacently awaiting them on a selected position which is in every way the best they have ever had.

As I write there is still much doubt as to whether the Germans will try and go further ahead here, for it is pretty clear that they are checked at this point, and that the Galician movement has reached its low-water mark as far as the Russians are concerned. The next blow will no doubt fall either north of Warsaw or possibly on the much-battered Bzura-Rawka Front itself, which for so many months has stood the wear and tear of many frantic efforts to break through.

CHAPTER XVI
THE FRONT OF IVANOV

Dated:
GALICIAN FRONTIER,
June 28, 1915.

IN Russia it is not a simple matter to change one's "front." For many months I have been associated with the group of armies over which Alexieff presides, where I have been able to move about from army to army with the utmost freedom. When I decided to change my base to the head-quarters of Ivanov and the front of Galicia I found myself surrounded by difficulties. For more than a month now, one could enter Warsaw without a permit or travel on the roads or pass to and from any of the towns in the area of war. I applied to my army friends in Warsaw and they, by permission of General Alexieff, kindly lent me a young officer whose duty it was to deliver me into the hands of the staff of the Galician Front.

We left Warsaw in my motor, not even knowing where the staff of Ivanov was, for at that moment it was on its way to a new destination, the retirements from Galicia having thrown the commanding General too far west to be conveniently in touch with his left flank armies. Stopping at a point about 100 versts from Warsaw, we learned our destination, and two days later motored into the quaint little Russian town not too far from Galicia, where the presiding genius of the Eastern Campaign had arrived that very morning with his whole staff. Here we found Ivanov living on a special train with his head-quarters in a kind of old museum. As the staff had just arrived, everything was still in confusion and nothing had been done to make the room, which was as large as a barn, comfortable. In the centre were two enormous tables covered with maps, before which sat a rather tired-looking man with a great full beard. He arose as we entered, and after shaking hands bade us be seated.

General Ivanov.

My car in a Galician village.

General Ivanov is a man of about sixty, with a kindly gentle face and a low
and musical voice. It is impossible to imagine him ever becoming excited or

ever making a sudden movement. Everything about him suggests calm, balance, poise and absolute self-control. As he speaks only Russian I was obliged to talk with him entirely through an interpreter. He has very deep blue eyes with a kindly little twinkle in them that one suspects might easily turn to a point of fire if he were roused. Since meeting him I have known many of his staff, and find that his personality is just what his appearance suggests. A great-hearted, kindly, unselfish man, he is worshipped by all whose duty it is to work with, for and under him. It is not etiquette according to the censor to quote anything that the General said, and I deeply regret this as I talked with him for an hour, and after the first thirty minutes felt as much at home as though I had known him a lifetime. His work and his army and the success of Russia make up his entire life. He impressed me as a big, earnest man, giving all the force of a powerful intellect to a very big job and doing it with the simplicity that is characteristic of all big men.

After a few commonplaces he asked me what I wanted. I told him quite frankly that from a news point of view, Russia, and the Galician campaign especially, was little known in the West. That the public in the West were depressed over the Russian reverses in Galicia, and that all of the friends of Russia wanted to know as accurately as possible what the conditions were in his armies. He leaned back in his chair and studied me closely for fully a minute, and then smiled a little, and the interpreter translated to me: "The General says that you may do what you like in his armies. He will detail an officer who speaks English to go with you. You may visit any army, any trench, any position or any organization that you wish, and he will give you the written permission. He will suggest a plan which he thinks advisable, but if you do not care for it you can make one up for yourself and he will give his consent to any programme that you care to suggest." The General smiled and then bent forward over his maps, and with his pencil pointed out to me the general arrangement of his armies, and after some discussion advised that I should start on his extreme left flank, the last division of which was operating in Bukovina not far from the Roumanian frontier. We were to stop as long as we cared to, and then visit each army in turn until we had covered all in his group, when the officer who was to be detailed to accompany us would deliver us to the first army next to him that belonged to the Alexieff group.

He then sent for the officer who was to be our guide, and presently there appeared a tall, handsome young man who was introduced to us as Prince Oblensky, a captain of the Chevalier Guards, now serving as personal aide-de-camp to General Ivanov. From the moment that we met him the Prince took charge of us completely, and for two weeks he was our guide, philosopher and friend. In passing I must say that I have never known a man of sweeter disposition and a more charming companion than this young

Captain, from whom I was not separated for above an hour or two at a time in fourteen days. The Prince took me around and introduced me to a number of the staff, and all of them talked freely and with very little reserve about the whole situation.

The point of view that I found at Ivanov's staff was this. Russia with her long front could not be strong everywhere at once. Her railroad system and her industrial organization were in no way equal to the German. Their sudden concentration was irresistible, and almost from the start the Russians realized that they would have to go back. It was hoped that the Germans could not maintain their ascendancy of ammunition and strength beyond the San. Indeed, for a few days there was something of a lull in which the Russians made gains in certain places. Then the flow of ammunition was resumed, and from that time it was pretty well understood that the Grodek line, and Lwow, would be held only as rearguard actions to delay the German advance, and to take from them the maximum loss at the minimum sacrifice. This particular staff, in whose hands rested the conduct of the whole manœuvre, had then the task of withdrawing these armies over this vast front in such order and symmetry that as they retired no one should overlap the flanks of the other, and that no loopholes should occur where an enemy could get through. With these numerous armies, operating in all kinds of countries with all sorts of lines of communications, falling back before fierce assaults from an enemy superior in guns and men, the performance of getting them safely back on to a united line where they could once more make a united stand, must, I think, take its place in history as one of the greatest military manœuvres that has ever been made.

I had just come from Petrograd where the greatest gloom prevailed in regard to the evacuation of Lwow, and I was surprised to find that no one here attached any great importance to Lwow. One officer of general's rank remarked, "We do not believe in holding untenable military positions for moral effect. Lwow is of no great value to us from a military point of view, and the way the line developed it was impossible to stay there without great risk. So we left. By and by we will go back and take it again when we have more ammunition." This was the first time that I heard this statement, but since then I have heard it at least a hundred times made by officers of all ranks from generals down to subalterns. All agreed that it was disappointing to come back after having fought so many months in taking Galicia, but I did not find one man who was in the least depressed; and from that day to this I have not heard in the army an expressed fear, or even a suggestion, that there might be a possibility that Russia would not prove equal to her task. The Russians as a race may be a bit slow in reaching conclusions, but once they get their teeth set I think there are no more stubborn or determined people in the world.

This retreat with all its losses and all its sacrifices has not, I think, shaken the courage of a single soldier in the whole Russian Army. They simply shut their teeth and pray for an opportunity to begin all over again. All eagerly assured me that the Germans and Austrians had lost far more than the Russians, and I was told by a high authority that the Germans estimated their own losses in two months at 380,000 killed, wounded and missing. One man significantly put the situation, "To judge of this movement one should see how it looks behind the German lines. In spite of their advances and bulletins of success, there has been great gloom behind their front. We know absolutely that every town and even every village in Eastern Silesia is filled with wounded, and in Breslau and Posen there is hardly a house that has not been requisitioned for the accommodation of wounded. Since the enemy crossed the Dunajec there has been an unbroken stream of wounded flowing steadily back across the frontier. *This* we do not see in the papers printed in Germany. The Russian game is to keep on weakening the Germans. We would rather advance, of course, but whether we advance or retreat we are weakening the enemy day after day; sometime he will be unable to repair his losses and then we will go on again. Do not worry. All of this is but temporary. We are not in the least discouraged."

Another statement which at first struck me as curious, but which I have since come to understand, was that the morale of the Austrians has been steadily decreasing since the capture of Przemysl and the fighting on the San. Since visiting Ivanov I have been in six armies and have talked in nearly all with the men who have been examining the Austrian prisoners. Their point of view seems to be pretty much the same. And when I say the Austrians, I mean, of course, the common soldiers and not the authorities or the officers. The Austrian soldiers' view is something like this: "We have fought now for a year, and in May we had practically lost Galicia. The end of the war, for which we have never cared, was almost in sight. We hoped that soon there would be some kind of peace and we could go home. We had lost Galicia, but the average man in the Austrian Army cares little for Galicia. Just as the end seemed in sight, the Germans, whom we don't like any way, came down here and dragged us along into this advance. At first we were pleased, but we never expected the Russians to hold out so long. Finally the Germans have given us back Lwow, and now little by little they are beginning to go away. It is only a question of time when they will all be gone either to France or against some other Russian front. Then the Russians will come back. Our officers will make us defend Lwow. They will make us defend the Grodek line, Przemysl and the Carpathians. The Russians are united. We are not. They will beat us as they did before. In the end we will be just where we were in May. It is all an extra fight, with more losses, more suffering and more misery. We owe it all to the Germans. We do not like it and we are not interested."

I think this point of view is more or less typical, and it accounts in a large measure for the fact that even though they are advancing the Austrians are still surrendering in enormous blocks whenever they get the chance of doing so without being caught in the act by their Allies.

For the most part the men that I talked with here thought that the army had retired about as far as it would for the present. But one feels constant surprise at the stoicism of the Russian, who does not apparently feel the smallest concern at withdrawals, for, as they say, "If they keep coming on into Russia it will be as it was with Napoleon. They can never beat us in the long run, and the further they force us back the worse for them. Look at Moscow," and they smile and offer you a cigarette. I have never in my life seen people who apparently have a more sublime confidence in their cause and in themselves than the Russians. Their confidence does not lie in their military technique, for I think all admit that in that the Germans are their superiors. It lies in their own confidence, in the stamina and character of the Russian people, who, when once aroused are as slow to leave off a fight as they are to begin it.

Throughout Russia to-day the strength of the war idea is growing daily. Every reverse, every withdrawal and every rumour of defeat only stiffens the determination to fight harder and longer. Time is their great ally they say, for Germany cannot, they are certain, fight indefinitely, while they believe that they can.

These opinions are not my own but the opinions of Russians. These men may be unduly enthusiastic about their countrymen, but what they say I have since heard all over the army at the Front; whether they are right or wrong they may certainly be taken as typical of the natural view.

When I left Petrograd I was not cheerful as to the outlook in Galicia. When I left Ivanov's head-quarters I felt more optimistic than I had been in six weeks.

CHAPTER XVII
HUNTING FOR THE ARMY OF THE BUKOVINA

Dated:

TLUST, GALICIA,

June 30, 1915.

THE town where General Ivanov lives is in Russia proper, and one may realize the scope of the military operations when one learns that the head-quarters of the army of his left flank is nearly 200 versts from the commander, while the furthest outpost of that army itself is perhaps 150 or 200 versts further still, which means that the directing genius is not far from 400 versts from his most distant line. After leaving the head-quarters we motored for 40 or 50 versts along the main line of communications of the whole group of armies, passing the usual endless train of transport and troops moving slowly forward to fill the ranks and replenish the supplies of the vast force that lies spread out ahead of us. For eleven months now, first in one part of Russia and then in another, I have been passing on the roads these endless chains of transport. Truly one begins to get the idea that there is nothing in the world nowadays but soldiers, guns, caissons and transport. One wonders where on earth it has all been kept in the days before August, a year ago, when a dozen transport carts or a battery of artillery was a sufficient novelty on the road to cause one to turn and look at it.

Forty versts from the head-quarters, we turn from the main road and strike off to the east and south toward Tarnopol, which though not the head-quarters of an army (if it were I could not mention it) is not too far away from the same. The road we follow is an excellent one as far as Kremenetz, a wonderfully picturesque little town tucked away in the hills, not far from the Russian-Galician frontier. Its quaint streets are now filled with the inevitable paraphernalia of war. From here by a road of lesser merit, we wind up a narrow road to one of the most picturesque spots I have ever seen, called Pochaief. This is the last town on the Russian side of the frontier. Here is a monastery a thousand years old, a Mecca to which come thousands of the devout peasantry from all over the Empire. The building itself is one of the greatest piles in Europe, and on its hill towers above the surrounding country so that it is visible for 20 versts with its golden dome shining in the summer sun. We reached the place late in the afternoon and learned that all the regular roads stopped here as it has apparently not been considered policy by either the Russian or Austrian Governments to have easy highways across the frontier. At this point we were perhaps 12 versts from the nearest good road in Galicia, a very trifling distance for a car that has been doing 70 or 80 versts an hour. The head of the police in Pochaief kindly lent us a gendarme, who assured us that we could get across the 12 intervening versts in an hour.

So with this placid-faced guide we started about nine in the evening. This amiable gendarme, who had more goodwill than brains, in half an hour had led us into a country of bluffs, forests, bridle paths and worse that defy description. I neglected to say that General Ivanov had kindly given us an extra motor to carry our baggage, and extra chauffeurs, etc. The moon was just rising and we were digging ourselves out of difficulties for the tenth time when our guide announced that the road was now a perfectly clear and good one, and saluting respectfully left us in the wood with our cars groaning and panting and staggering over bumps and ditches until one came to have the most intense admiration for the gentlemen that design motor-cars. It is a mystery to me how they ever stand the misery that they have to undergo.

By midnight we were sitting out on a ridge of hills stuck fast in a field with our engines racing, and the mud flying and the whole party pushing and sweating and swearing. No doubt our guide had foreseen this very spot and had had the discretion to withdraw before we reached it. This was the exact frontier, and with its rolling hills and forests stretching before us in the quiet moonlight it was very beautiful. Our Prince, who never gets discouraged or ruffled, admired the scenery and smoked a cigarette, and we all wished for just one moment of our guide, for whom we had sundry little pleasantries prepared. While we were still panting and gasping, a figure on horseback came over the hill and cautiously approached us. He proved to be a policeman from the Galician side who had come out as the Prince told us because he had heard our engines and thought that a German aeroplane "had sat down on the hill" and he had come out to capture it. He was slightly disappointed at his mistake, but guided us back to the village whence he had come. Near here we found a beautiful Austrian estate, where we woke up the keeper and made him give us "my lady's" bed chamber for the night, which he did grudgingly.

Our troubles were now over, for after one breakdown in the morning we were on a good highway which ran *viâ* Potkaimen down to Tarnopol. At Potkaimen we were again on the line of travel, with the line of creaking transport and jangling guns and caissons. I have never passed through a more beautiful or picturesque country in my life, and wonder why tourists do not come this way. Apparently until the war these villages were as much off the beaten path as though they were in the heart of Africa. Rolling hills, forests, with silvery lakes dotting the valleys, extend for miles with wonderful little streams watering each small water-shed between the ridges. The roads are fine, and the last 60 versts into Tarnopol we made in record time. A few miles from the city we began to pass an endless line of carts bearing all sorts and descriptions of copper. It was evident that many distilleries and other plants had been hurriedly dismantled, and everything in them containing copper shipped away less it fall into the hands of the copper-hungry enemy.

Here, too, we passed long lines of the carts of the Galician peasantry fleeing from the fear of the German invasion. It strikes one as extraordinary that these inhabitants, many of whose husbands, brothers and fathers are fighting in the Austrian Armies, should take refuge in flight at the rumour of their approach. It is a sad commentary on the reputation of the Germans that even the peoples of their Allies flee at the report of their approach. The name of Prussian down here seems to carry as much terror to the Galician peasant as ever it did to the Belgians or the Poles in other theatres of war. The peasantry are moving out bag and baggage with all the pathos and misery which the abandonment of their homes and lifelong treasures spells to these simple folk. Even ten months' association with similar scenes does not harden one to the pitifulness of it all. Little children clinging to their toys, mothers, haggard and frightened, nursing babes at their breasts, and fathers and sons urging on the patient, weary, family horse as he tugs despairingly at the overloaded cart weighted down with the pathetic odds and ends of the former home.

Tarnopol itself was a great surprise to me. It is a typical Austrian town with a lovely park in the centre and three hotels which are nearly first class. Paved streets, imposing public buildings and a very fine station, besides hundreds of lovely dwelling houses, make a very beautiful little town; and with its setting in the valley, Tarnopol seems an altogether desirable place. Here as elsewhere troops are seething. The station is a military restaurant and emergency hospital combined. One of the waiting-rooms has been turned into an operating and dressing-room, and when there is fighting on at the front the whole place is congested with stretchers and the atmosphere reeks of disinfectants and ether fumes.

We stopped here only overnight, for we are bound to the furthest stretch of our front to the south-east. In the evening there came through battalion after battalion of troops swinging through the streets, tired, dirty and battle stained, but, with it all, singing at the top of their lungs. These men were moving from one front to another, and most of them had been fighting for weeks. The first glance was sufficient to make one realize that these troops were certainly not down-hearted.

In strong contrast to the Russians was the sight of the latest haul of prisoners which passed through the next morning—several thousand Austrians and two or three hundred Germans.

In spite of their being caught at the hightide of their advance movement the Austrians had the same broken-hearted expression that I have seen in tens of thousands of Austrian prisoners for ten months. I have now seen Austrians from every quarter of their Empire, and I must say I have never seen a squad of prisoners who have not had the same expression of hopelessness and resignation. These were well-clothed and for prisoners moderately clean. The critic may say that prisoners always look depressed and dejected, but to judge the Austrians, one must compare them with the Germans, and it was possible to do so on this occasion, for directly behind the troops of the Hapsburgs came two or three hundred Germans. I have never seen such spectacles in my life. Worn, haggard, ragged and tired they were, but in contrast to the Austrians, they walked proudly, heads thrown back, glaring defiantly at the curious crowds that watched them pass. Whether they are prisoners or conquerors the German soldiers always wear the same mien of superiority and arrogance. But the significance of this group was not their self-respect and defiance of their captivity but their condition. I have never in war seen men so nearly "all-in" as these prisoners. Two in the line had no shirts, their ragged coats covering their bare, brown breasts. Some had no hats, all were nearly in rags, the boots of many were worn thin and many of them limped wearily. Boys of eighteen marched by men who looked a hundred, though I suppose they were under fifty actually. One saw a giant of 6 feet 5 inches walking by a stripling of 5 feet 2 inches. Their faces were thin and drawn, and many of them looked as if one might have hung hats on their cheek-bones. These men may be wrong and they may be cruel, but one must admit that they are object lessons in fortitude, and whatever they are they are certainly soldiers. In wagons behind came wounded Germans, mostly privates. Later I discovered that a number of these troops had just come from the French front. As one said, "Arrived at noon, captured at three." Their explanation of their capture was that their officer lost the way. Further examination brought forth the information that nearly all their officers had been killed; and that the bulk of the company officers were now either young boys or old men who knew little of maps or military matters, which accounted for them getting lost and falling into the Russian hands. The Austrians were captured because, as usual, they wanted to be. The numbers of the prisoners seen here, that is 2,000 Austrians and 200 Germans, is just about the proportion in which morale and enthusiasm in the war exists in the two armies.

Next morning having obtained the necessary permits we took our motors and headed south for the army lying on the Dniester with its flank in the Bukovina.

CHAPTER XVIII
THE RUSSIAN LEFT

GERMANIKOWKA, GALICIA,
July 3, 1915.

THE army of the Bukovina, or the extreme Russian left, is probably the most romantic organization operating in one of the most picturesque countries in the whole theatre of this gigantic war. In the first place the left is composed very largely of the type of cavalry which I think no other country in the world can duplicate, that is the irregular horsemen brought from all parts of the East. Tribes from the Caucasus, Tartars, Mongols, and I know not what others, are here welded together into brigades and divisions, and make, all told, nearly two complete army corps with only a sprinkling of infantry and regular cavalry. It was this army that gained such headway in its advance toward the Hungarian plain, and it is this very army that is credited with so alarming the Hungarians that they threatened independent peace unless something was done for them. That something we know now was Austria's wail to Germany and the resulting Galician campaign.

During all the first part of the great German drive, this army with its hordes of wild cavalry was proceeding confidently "hacking its way through" all resistance, and capturing thousands upon thousands of Austrians or Hungarians that came in its way. For nearly a month after things were going badly in the West, it was moving victoriously forward until it became evident that unless it stopped it would find itself an independent expedition headed for Buda-Pest and completely out of touch with the rest of the Russian line which was withdrawing rapidly. Then came a pause, and as the flanking armies continued to retreat, the army was very unwillingly obliged to retire also to keep in touch with its neighbour. My own impression as to the spirits of this army, especially of the cavalry corps, is similar to the impression one forms when one sees a bulldog being let loose from another hound whom he has down, and is chewing luxuriously when his master comes along, and drags him away on a leash. So these troops have retired snarling and barking over their shoulders, hoping that the enemy would follow close enough to let them have another brush with them.

G. H. Mewes.

There has been fighting of more or less acuteness, especially where German troops have been engaged, but taken on the whole this portion of the Russian front cannot be considered a serious one and their withdrawal has been forced by the greater strategy. I found many of the younger officers of the opinion that they could advance at any time if they only had the permission from the powers that be. As for the soldiers—a single look into those set swarthy faces was enough to satisfy one that they would willingly advance in any event regardless of policy or orders either. I have never seen such fierce looking men in my life. Many of them do not speak Russian, and to them the war is a real joy. Heretofore they have had to be content to fight among themselves for nothing in particular; now that they have a chance to fight for something really great they are in their element. I question how valuable troops of this character would be under different conditions, but here in this rough Bukovina country they are nearly ideal for their work, as is manifest from the manner in which they have swept the enemy before them.

On leaving Tarnopol we came directly to the head-quarters of one of these corps, where we spent three extremely interesting days. The position which this army was holding is, in a rough way, from the junction of the Zota Lipa and the Dniester, down that river to a point perhaps 20 versts west of Chocin, and thence in an irregular line 40 or 50 versts through Bukovina in the direction of the Roumanian frontier. The Dniester itself is a deep-flowing river lying between great bluffs which for miles skirt the river bank on both sides. These bluffs are for the most part crested with heavy timber. In a general way the Russians are holding one bank, and the Austrians the other, though here and there patches of Russians have clung to the South side, while in one or two spots Austrians backed by Germans have gained a foothold on the north bank. The first afternoon I arrived, I went out to a 356 metre hill from where I could look over the whole country. I discerned easily the lines of the Austrian and Russian positions between which was the valley through which flowed the Dniester. There are any number of young Petrograd swells here who have left their crack cavalry corps, many of which are dismounted and fighting in the trenches in Poland and on other fronts, to put on the uniform of the Cossack and lead these rough riders of the East in their romantic sweeps towards the Hungarian plains. I have been in some armies where I found hardly any one who spoke English, but in this one corps I found nearly a score who spoke it, many as well as I did, which indicates pretty clearly the type of young men that Russia has here, and is one reason, no doubt, why the army has done so well.

Stanley Washburn, Prince Oblensky, Count Tolstoy, Count Keller.

Here I met Count Tolstoi, son of the novelist; Count Keller, whose father was killed by Japanese shrapnel on the Motienling Pass in Manchuria, and many other men whose names are well known in Russia. Count Keller was the ranking Captain in a squadron (*sotnia*, I believe they call it) of cavalry from the Caucasus, and carried us off to his lair in a valley not far from the Dniester. Here we met a courteous old Persian who commanded the regiment, and dined in a quaint old castle where they had their head-quarters. Deep in its little valley, the castle was not seen by the Austrians, but had long since been spotted by the aeroplanes of the enemy. The result was that every afternoon a few shells were sent over the southern ridge of hills, just to let the regimental staff know that they were not forgotten. The day before we arrived twelve horses were killed in the garden, and while we were cleaning up for dinner, a shrapnel shell whined through the yard bursting somewhere off in the brush.

After dinner the dancers of the regiment came up and in the half-light performed their weird evolutions. In long flowing coats, with their oriental faces, emitting uncanny sounds from their mouths, they formed a picture that I shall long remember. Count Keller told me that in spite of all their wildness they were fine troops to command, for, as he said, "They have very high ideals of their profession. I may be killed or wounded, but I am always sure that my men will never leave me. They cannot speak my tongue, but there is not a man in my command who would not feel himself permanently disgraced if he left the body of his officer on the field of battle. They are absolutely fearless and will go anywhere, caring nothing whatever for death, wounds, hardship or anything else that war brings forth. I am very fond of them indeed."

The positions at this point were about three versts distant from our little isolated valley, and as they were out on the crest of the bluff it was impossible to visit them until after dark. So on the great veranda of the castle we sat late after our dinner, until darkness fell and a great full moon rose slowly above the neighbouring hills flooding the valley with its silver rays, bringing out the old white castle as clearly in the darkness as a picture emerges from a photographic plate when the developer is poured upon it. It was just after midnight when Count Keller and I, well mounted on Cossack ponies, rode down into the valley and turned our horses on to the winding road that runs beside the little stream that leaps and gurgles over the rocks on the way to the Dniester. For a mile or more we followed the river, and then turning sharply to the right, took a bridle path and climbed slowly up the sharp side of the bluff. For fifteen or twenty minutes we rode through the woods, now in the shadow and now out in an opening where the shadows of the branches swaying softly in the moonlight made patterns on the road. Suddenly we came out upon a broad white road where the Count paused.

"We are advised to leave the horses here," he remarked casually, "Shall we go on? Are you afraid?" Not knowing anything about the position I had no ideas on the subject, so we continued down the moonlit road, and while I was wondering where we were, we came out abruptly on the bluff just above the river, where the great white road ran along the crest for a mile or more. I paused for a moment to admire the view. Deep down below us, like a ribbon of silver in the shimmering moonlight, lay the great river. Just across on the other bank was the Austrian line with here and there spots of flickering light where the Austrians had fires in their trenches. There was not a sound to mar the silence of the perfect night save the gentle rustle of the wind in the trees. "The Austrians can see us plainly from here," remarked the Count indifferently. "Gallop!" The advice seemed sound to me, but not knowing the country I was obliged to reply, "Which way?" "Right," he replied laconically.

It is sufficient to say that I put spurs to my horse, and for the mile that lay exposed in the moonlight my little animal almost flew while the Count pounded along a close second just behind me. A mile away we reached the welcome shadows of a small bunch of trees, and as I rode into the wood I was sharply challenged by a guttural voice, and as I pulled my horse up on his haunches a wild-looking Cossack took my bridle. Before I had time to begin an explanation, the Count came up and the sharp words of the challenge were softened to polite speeches of welcome from the officer in command.

We were in the front line trench or rather just behind it, for the road lay above it while the trench itself was between it and the river where it could command the crossing with its fire. Here as elsewhere, I found men who could speak English, the one an officer and the other a man in charge of a machine gun. This man had been five years in Australia and had come back to "fight the Germans," as he said. For an hour we sat up on the crest of the trench under the shadow of a tree, and watched in the sky the flare of a burning village to our right, which was behind the Russian lines, and had been fired just at dark by Austrian shells. I found that all the Russians spoke well of the Austrians. They said they were kindly and good-natured, never took an unfair advantage, lived up to their flags of truce, etc. Their opinion of the Germans was exactly the opposite. One man said, "Sometimes the Austrians call across that they won't shoot during the night. Then we all feel easy and walk about in the moonlight. One of our soldiers even went down and had a bathe in the river, while the Austrians called across to him jokes and remarks, which of course he could not understand. The Germans say they won't fire, and just as soon as our men expose themselves they begin to shoot. They are always that way."

Cossacks dancing the Tartars' native dance.

I have never known a more absolutely quiet and peaceful scene than this from the trench on the river's bluff. As I was looking up the streak of silver below us, thinking thus, there came a deep boom from the east and then another and another, and then on the quiet night the sharp crackle of the machine guns and the rip and roar of volley firing. It was one of those spasms of fighting that ripple up and down a line every once in a while, but after a few minutes it died away, the last echoes drifting away over the hills, and silence again reigned over the Dniester. The fire in the village was burning low, and the first grey streaks of dawn were tinging the horizon in the east when we left the trench, and by a safer bridle path returned to the castle and took our motor-car for head-quarters which we reached just as the sun was rising.

The positions along this whole front are of natural defence and have received and required little attention. Rough shelter for the men, and cover for the machine guns is about all that any one seems to care for here. The fighting is regarded by these wild creatures as a sort of movable feast, and they fight now in one place and now in another. Of course they have distinctive lines of trenches, though they cannot compare with the substantial works that one finds in the Bzura-Rawka lines and the other really serious fronts in Poland and elsewhere. In a general way it matters very little whether the army moves forward or backward just here. The terrain for 100 versts is adapted to defence, and the army can, if it had to do so, go back so far without yielding to the enemy anything that would have any important bearing on the campaign of the Russian Army as a whole. From the first day that I joined this army, I felt the conviction that it could be relied upon to take care of itself, and that its retirements or changes of front could be viewed with something approaching to equanimity.

CHAPTER XIX
WITH A RUSSIAN CAVALRY CORPS

ON THE DNIESTER,
July 4, 1915.

IT would not be in the least difficult for me to write a small volume on my impressions and observations during the time that I was with this particular cavalry corps on the Dniester; but one assumes that at this advanced period in the war, readers are pretty well satiated with descriptive material of all sorts, and there is so much news of vital importance from so many different fronts, that the greatest merit of descriptive writing in these days no doubt lies in its brevity. I will therefore cut as short as possible the account of my stay in this very interesting organization.

The General in command was a tough old cavalry officer who spoke excellent English. He was of the type that one likes to meet at the Front, and his every word and act spoke of efficiency and of the soldier who loves his profession. His head-quarters were in a little dirty village, and his rooms were in the second story of an equally unpretentious building. The room contained a camp-bed and a group of tables on which were spread the inevitable maps of the positions. This particular General as far as I could gather spent about one half of each day poring over his maps, and the other half in visiting his positions. Certainly he seemed to know every foot of the terrain occupied by his command, and every by-path and crossroad seemed perfectly familiar to him. Without the slightest reservation (at least as far as I could observe) he explained to me his whole position, pointing it out on the map. When he began to talk of his campaign he immediately became engrossed in its intricacies. Together we pored over his map. "You see," he said, "I have my — brigade here. To the left in the ravine I have one battery of big guns just where I can use them nicely. Over here you see I have a bridge and am across the river. Now the enemy is on this side here (and he pointed at a blue mark on the map) but I do not mind; if he advances I shall give him a push here (and again he pointed at another point on the map), and with my infantry brigade I shall attack him just here, and as you see he will have to go back"; and thus for half an hour he talked of the problems that were nearest and dearest to his heart. He was fully alive to the benefits that publicity might give an army, and did everything in his power to make our visit as pleasant and profitable as possible.

H.I.H. The Grand Duke Michael Alexandrovitch, Commander of two divisions of Cossacks.

On the afternoon of the second day Prince Oblensky arranged for us to meet the Grand Duke Michael who is commanding a division of Caucasian cavalry, one of whose detachments we visited in the trenches a few nights ago. I should say he is not much over forty years of age, and he is as unaffected and democratic a person as one can well imagine. I talked with him for nearly an hour on the situation, not only on his immediate front but in the theatre of the war as a whole. Like everyone in Russian uniform whom I have met, he was neither depressed nor discouraged, but evinced the same stubborn optimism that one finds everywhere in the Russian army. As one saw him in his simple uniform with nothing to indicate his rank but shoulder straps of the same material as his uniform, and barring the Cross of St. George (won by his personal valour on the field of battle) without a decoration, it was strange to think that this man living so simply in a dirty village in this far fringe of the Russian Front, might have been the Czar of all the Russias, living in the Winter Palace in Petrograd, but for a few years in time of birth. The Western World likes to think of Russia as an autocracy, with its nobility living a life apart surrounded by form and convention, but now, at any rate, I think there is no country in the world where the aristocracy are more democratic than in Russia. It is true that the Czar himself is inaccessible, but he is about the only man in Russia who is; and even he, when one does meet him, is as simple, unaffected and natural as any ordinary gentleman in England or in America.

From the Grand Duke's head-quarters I motored out to the Staff of a Cavalry Brigade, and had tea with the General who, after entertaining us with a dance performed by a group of his tamed "wild men," went himself with us to his front line trench. His head-quarters were near the front, so near in fact that while we were waiting for the dancers to appear, a big shell fell in a field just across the way, with a report that sent the echoes rolling away over hill and valley. It is considered bad form to notice these interruptions however, and no one winked an eye or took any notice of the incident. The General's trenches were not unlike those I had already before visited, except that one could get into them in the daytime without risk of being shot at if one came up through the woods, which ran rather densely to the very crest of the bluff.

Here was the most curious sight that I have ever seen in war. The rough-and-ready cavalrymen from the Caucasus with their great caps, each as big as a bushel basket, all covered with wool about six inches long, were lying about behind small earthworks on the fringe of the woods peering along their rifle barrels which were pointed across the river. On an almost similar elevation on the opposite side was the line of the Austrian trenches. For once the sun was over our shoulders, and in their eyes and not ours, so that I could safely walk to the edge of the wood and study their works through my field glasses. Everything was very quiet this particular afternoon, and I could see the blue-coated figures of the enemy moving about behind their own trenches, as indeed the Russians could with their naked eyes. The war has lasted so long now, and the novelty has so worn off, that it is safe to do many things that could not have been done in the early months. No one nowadays is anxious to start anything unnecessary, and sniping is a bore to all concerned, and it hardly draws a shot if one or two men are seen moving about. It is only when important groups appear that shots are fired.

Not two hundred yards back in the woods were the bivouacs of the reserves, and the hundreds and hundreds of the little ponies tethered to trees. There they stood dozing in the summer sunshine, twitching their tails and nipping each other occasionally. I have never seen cavalry in the trenches before, much less cavalry with their horses so near that they could actually wait until the enemy were almost in their works and then mount and be a mile away before the trench itself was occupied. In this rough country where the positions lend themselves to this sort of semi-regular work, I dare say these peculiar types of horsemen are extremely effective, though I question if they would appear to the same advantage in other parts of the Russian operations. As a matter of fact one of the regiments now here was formerly attached to the Warsaw Front, but was subsequently removed from that army and sent down to Bukovina as a place more suited to its qualities.

We had a bit of bad luck on this position with our motor-car which we had left in a dip behind the line. Just as we were ready to start for home, there came a sharp rainstorm which so wetted the roads that the hill we had come down so smoothly on dry soil proved impossible to go up when wet. A *sotnia* of Cossacks pulled us out of our first mess with shouts and hurrahs, but when night fell we found ourselves in another just as bad a few hundreds yards further along. For an hour we went through the misery of spinning wheels and racing engines without effect. We had stopped, by bad luck, in about the only place where the road was visible from the Austrian lines, but as it was dark they could not see us. When the chauffeur lighted his lamps, however, three shells came over from the enemy, extinguishing the lamps. About ten in the evening we started on foot, and walked to a point where we borrowed a car from the brigade staff, and went on home. Our own car was extricated at daylight by a band of obliging Cossacks who had been on duty all night in the trenches, and were going into the reserve for a day's rest.

Leaving this army corps in the afternoon we motored further east, and paid our respects to a brigade of the regular cavalry, composed of the —th Lancers and the — Hussars, both crack cavalry regiments of the Russian army, and each commanded by officers from the Petrograd aristocracy. The brigade had been in reserve for three days, and as we saw it was just being paraded before its return to the trenches. The —th Lancers I had seen before in Lwow just after the siege of Przemysl, in which they took part, at that time fighting in the trenches alongside of the infantry. I have never seen mounts in finer condition, and I believe there is no army on any of the fronts where this is more typical than in the Russian. On this trip I have been in at least fifteen or twenty cavalry units, and, with one exception, I have not seen anywhere horses in bad shape; the exception had been working overtime for months without chance to rest or replace their mounts. The Colonel of the Lancers I had known before in Lwow, and he joined me in my motor and rode with me the 20 versts to the position that his cavalry was going to relieve at that time. This gentleman was an ardent cavalryman and had served during the greater part of the Manchurian campaign. To my surprise I found that he had been in command of a squadron of Cossacks that came within an ace of capturing the little town of Fakumen where was Nogi's staff; and he was as much surprised to learn that I was attached to Nogi's staff there as correspondent for an American paper.

The Colonel was now in charge of the Lancer regiment and was, as I learned, a great believer in the lance as a weapon. "Other things being equal," he told me, "I believe in giving the soldiers what they want. They do want the lance, and this is proved by the fact that in this entire campaign not one of my troopers has lost his lance. The moral effect is good on our troops, for it gives them confidence, and it is bad on the enemy, for it strikes terror into their hearts. Before this war it was supposed that cavalry could never get near infantry. My regiment has twice attacked infantry and broken them up both times. In both cases they broke while we were still three or four hundred yards distant, and of course the moment they broke they were at our mercy."

For an hour or more we motored over the dusty roads before we dipped over a crest and dropped down into a little village not far from the Dniester, where were the head-quarters of the regiment that the Lancers were coming in to relieve. As we turned the corner of the village street a shrapnel shell burst just to the south of us, and I have an idea that someone had spotted our dust as we came over the crest.

The cavalry here was a regiment drawn from the region of the Amur river, and as they were just saddling up preparatory to going back into reserve for a much-needed rest, I had a good chance to note the condition of both men and mounts, which were excellent. The latter were Siberian ponies, which make, I think, about the best possible horses for war that one can find. They are tough, strong, live on almost anything, and can stand almost any extremes of cold or heat without being a bit the worse for it. These troops have had, I suppose, as hard work as any cavalry in the Russian Army, yet the ponies were as fat as butter and looked as contented as kittens. The Russians everywhere I have seen them are devoted to their horses, and what I say about the condition of the animals applies not only to the cavalry but even to the transport, to look at which, one would never imagine that we were in the twelfth month of war. The Colonel of the Amur Cavalry gave us tea and begged us to stay on, but as it was getting late and the road we had to travel was a new one to us, and at points ran not far from the lines of the enemy, we deemed it wiser to be on our way. Some sort of fight started after dark, and to the south of us, from the crests of the hills that we crossed, we could see the flare of the Austrian rockets and the occasional jagged flash of a bursting shell; further off still the sky was dotted with the glow of burning villages. In fact for the better part of the week I spent in this vicinity I do not think that there was a single night that one could not count fires lighted by the shells from the artillery fire.

Midnight found us still on the road, but our Prince, who was ever resourceful, discovered the estate of an Austrian noble not far from the main road, and we managed to knock up the keeper and get him to let us in for the night. The Count who owned the place was in the Austrian Army, and the Countess was in Vienna.

The Russian soldier at meal-time. Ten men share the soup, which is served in a huge pan.

Leaving this place early the following morning we started back for Tarnopol and the Headquarters of the Army that stands second in the Russian line of battle counting from the left flank.

CHAPTER XX
ON THE ZOTA LIPA

TARNOPOL,
July 6, 1915.

WE found the General of the army now occupying the line that runs from approximately the head of the Zota Lipa to its confluence with the Dniester, living in a palace south-west of ———. These wonderful estates come as a great surprise to strangers travelling through the country. One passes a sordid Galician village filled with dogs and half-naked children, and perhaps on the outskirts one comes to a great gate and turning in finds oneself in a veritable Versailles, with beautiful avenues of trees, lakes, waterfalls and every other enhancement of the landscape that money and good taste can procure. I have never seen more beautiful grounds or a more attractively decorated and beautifully furnished house than this one where our particular General was living with his staff.

During my visit to this army, I saw and talked with the General commanding twice, and he permitted me to see his maps and gave his consent to my visiting any of his line which I desired to see. He sent one of his staff with me, who spoke English, as a guide and interpreter. Again I regret I cannot give the General's name, but suffice to say that from this head-quarters I gathered that, barring the failure of their centre army, a retreat would probably have been unnecessary, though it is folly to disguise the fact that this army was hard pressed, suffered not a little, and was constantly outnumbered in both men and munitions. It is probably not unfair to place its whole movement under the category of a rear-guard action.

During the retreat from Stryj to the Zota Lipa, where the army was when I visited it, captures of enemy prisoners were made to the number of 53,000, as I was informed by the highest authority. The bulk of these were Austrians. As I said at the time, I incline to think this must be considered one of the most remarkable retreats in history. If I was disposed to doubt this statement when I first heard it, my hesitation vanished, when, during three days, I personally saw between 4,000 and 5,000 Austrian prisoners that had been taken within a week, regardless of the fact that the army was still retiring before the enemy. I think that the mere mention of the matter of prisoners is enough to convince the reader that this army was not a demoralized one, and that the furthest stretch of imagination could not consider it a badly defeated one. A glance at the map serves to show that the country, from the beginning of this retreat to the Zota Lipa, is an ideal one in which to fight defensively! and as a matter of fact the country for 100 versts further east is equally well adapted to the same purpose. A number of streams running

- 134 -

almost due north and south flow into the Dniester river, and as each of these rivulets runs between more or less pretentious bluffs it is a very simple matter to hold them with very little fieldworks.

What the Russians have been doing here is this. They take up one of these natural lines of defence and throw up temporary works on the bluffs and wait for the Austrians. When the latter come up they find the Russians too strong to be turned out with anything short of the full enemy strength. Usually a week is taken up by the Austro-German forces in bringing up their full strength, getting their guns in position and preparing for an attack. The Russians in the meantime sit on their hills, taking all the losses that they can get, and repel the Austrian preliminary attacks as long as they can do so without risking too much. By the time that enemy operations have reached a really serious stage, and an attack in force is made, it is discovered that the main force of the Russians has departed, and when the positions are finally carried, only a rearguard of cavalry is discovered holding the trenches; the bulk of these usually get away on their horses, leaving the exhausted Austrians sitting in a hardly-won line with the knowledge that the Russians are already miles away waiting for them to repeat the operation all over again. The prisoners have been captured for the most part in preliminary operations on these works, on occasions where the Russians have made counter attacks or where the Austrians have advanced too far and been cut off. The youth and inexperience of their officers, and the fact that the rank and file have no heart in the fight, have made it easy for them to go too far in the first place, and willing to surrender without a fight when they discover their mistake. All of this I was told at head-quarters, and had an opportunity to verify the next day by going to one of the forward positions on the Zota Lipa.

I have within the last few months, after poking about on the billiard table terrain of the Polish Front, acquired a great liking for hills, protected by woods if possible. I have therefore picked places on this trip where I could get to points of observation from which I could see the terrain without being, shot at, if this could be avoided with dignity. It was just such a place as this towards which we headed the next day. My own impressions were, and still are, that this army might retire further yet from its present positions. There are certain reasons which I cannot divulge at present, but are no doubt understood in England, that makes it unwise for these armies to attempt to hold advance positions if they can fall quietly back without the sacrifice of any positions which will have a bad effect on the Russian campaign as a whole. This particular army with its neighbour to the south can do this for more than 100 versts without materially impairing its own *moral*, and, as far as I can see, without giving the enemy any other advantage than something to talk about.

On the way out to the positions I passed important bodies of troops "changing front," for it is hardly possible to call what I witnessed, a retreat. They came swinging down the road laughing, talking and then singing at the top of their lungs. Had I not known the points of the compass, I should have concluded that they had scored a decisive victory and were marching on the capital of the enemy. But of such stuff are the moujik soldiers of the Czar.

We first visited the head-quarters of one of the Army corps, and then motored through Ztoczow, a very beautiful little Austrian town lying just at the gateway between ridges of hills that merge together as they go eastward, making the road climb to the plateau land which, indented by the valleys of the rivers running into the Dniester, stretches practically for 100 versts east of here. Turning south from the little town we climbed up on to this plateau land, and motored for 15 or 20 versts south to the head-quarters of a General commanding a division of Cossack cavalry from the Caucasus. With him we had tea, and as he spoke excellent English I was able to gather much of interest from his point of view. He was not sufficiently near head-quarters nor of rank high enough to be taken into the higher councils, and therefore did not know the reasons for the constant retirements. Again and again he assured me that the positions now held could as far as he was concerned be retained indefinitely. His was the thankless job of the rear guard, and it apparently went against his fighting instincts to occupy these splendid positions and then retire through some greater strategy, which he, far off in the woods from everything, did not understand.

One is constantly impressed with the isolation of the men holding important minor commands. For days and weeks they are without outside news, and many of them have even only a vague idea as to what is going on in neighbouring corps, and almost none at all of the movements in adjoining armies. I was convinced from the way this General—and he was a fine old type—talked, that he did not consider his men had ever been beaten at all, and that he looked upon his movements merely as the result of orders given for higher strategic considerations. From him we went out to the line on the Zota Lipa. The Russians at this time had retired from the Gnita Lipa (the great Austro-German "victory" where they lost between 4,000 and 5,000 prisoners and I know not how many dead and wounded) and had now for four days been quietly sitting on the ridges of the second Lipa waiting for the enemy to come up. I think no army can beat the Russians when it comes to forced marches, and after each of these actions they have retired in two days a distance that takes the enemy four or five to cover. It is because of this speed of travel that there have been stragglers, and it is of such that the enemy have taken the prisoners of whom they boast so much. The position we visited was on a wonderful ridge crested with woods. The river lay so deeply in its little valley that, though but a mile away, we could not see the water at all, but only the shadow wherein it lay. Our trenches were just on the edge of it while our guns and reserves were behind us. From our position we could look into the rear of our trenches, and across the river where the country was more open and where the Austrians were just beginning to develop their advance. Though the Russians had been here for several days, the enemy was just coming up now and had not yet brought up his guns at all.

Our infantry were sniping at the blue figures which dotted the wood a verst or two away, but at such a range that its effect was not apparent. Our guns had not yet fired a shot, and hence the Austrians knew nothing of our position but the fact that they were in contact with snipers in some sort of a trench. In any case the Austrians in a thin blue line which one could see with the naked eye, were busily digging a trench across a field just opposite us and about 4,000 metres distant, while with my glasses I could see the blue-clad figures slipping about on the fringe of the wood behind their trench diggers. Our observation point was under a big tree on an advanced spur of the hill, a position which I think would not be held long after the arrival of the Austrian guns. The battery commander had screwed his hyperscope into the tree trunk, and was hopping about in impatience because his field wire had not yet come up from the battery position in the rear. He smacked his lips with anticipation as he saw the constantly, increasing numbers of the enemy parading about opposite without any cover, and at frequent intervals kept sending messengers to hurry on the field telegraph corps.

Cavalry taking up position.

Russian band playing the men to the trenches.

In a few minutes there came a rustle in the brush, and two soldiers with a reel unwinding wire came over the crest, and dropping on their knees behind some bushes a few yards away, made a quick connection with the telephone instrument, and then announced to the commander that he was in touch with his guns. Instantly his face lit up, but before speaking he turned and took a squint through his hyperscope; then with clenched fist held at arms length he made a quick estimate of the range and snapped out an order over his shoulder. The orderly at the 'phone mumbled something into the mouthpiece of the instrument. "All ready," he called to the commander. "Fire," came the quick response. Instantly there came a crash from behind us. I had not realized that the guns were so near until I heard the report and the shell whine over our heads. We stood with our glasses watching the Austrians. A few seconds later came the white puff in the air appearing suddenly as from nowhere, and then the report of the explosion drifted back to us on the breeze. The shot was high and over. Another quick order, and another screamed over our head, this time bursting well in front of the trench.

Through my glasses I could see that there was some agitation among the blue figures in the field across the river. Again the gun behind us snapped out its report, and this time the shell burst right over the trench and the diggers disappeared as by magic, and even the blue coats on the edge of the wood suddenly vanished from our view. The artillery officer smiled quietly, took another good look through the glass at his target, called back an order, and the battery came into action with shell after shell breaking directly over the trench. But as far as we could see there was not a living soul, only the dark brown ridge where lay the shallow ditch which the Austrians had been digging. The value of the shrapnel was gone, and the Captain sighed a little as he called for his carefully saved and precious high-explosives, of which as I learned he had very few to spare. The first fell directly in an angle of the trench, and burst with the heavy detonation of the higher explosive, sending up a little volcano of dust and smoke, while for a minute the hole smoked as though the earth were on fire.

"They are in that place right enough," was the verdict of the director, "I saw them go. I'll try another," and a second later another shell burst in almost the identical spot. That it had found a living target there could be no doubt, for suddenly the field was dotted with the blue coats scampering in all directions for the friendly shelter of the wood in their rear. It was an object lesson of the difference in effectiveness between high explosive and shrapnel. The Captain laughed gleefully at his success as he watched the effect of his practice. Nearly all the Austrians were running, but away to the right was a group of five, old timers perhaps who declined to run, and they strolled leisurely away in the manner of veterans who scorn to hurry. The Commander again held out his fist, made a quick estimate of the range and called a deviation of target and a slight elevation of the gun. Again the gun crashed behind us and I saw the shell fall squarely in the centre of the group. From the smoking crater three figures darted at full speed. I saw nothing of the other two. No doubt their fragments lay quivering in the heap of earth and dust from which the fumes poured for fully a minute. It was excellent practice, and when I congratulated the officer he smiled and clicked his heels as pleased as a child. We saw nothing more of the enemy while we remained. No doubt they were waiting for the night to come to resume their digging operations.

How long the Russians will remain on this line can be merely speculation. Many of these lines that are taken up temporarily prove unusually strong, or the enemy proves unexpectedly weak, and what was intended as only a halt, gradually becomes strengthened until it may become the final line. My own idea was, however, that after forcing the Austrians to develop their full strength and suffer the same heavy losses, the Russians would again retire to a similar position and do it all over again. It is this type of action which is slowly breaking the hearts of the enemy. Again and again they are forced into these actions which make them develop their full strength and are taken only when supported by their heavy guns, only to find, when it is all over, that the Russians have departed and are already complacently awaiting them a few days' marches further on. This kind of game has already told heavily on the

Austrian spirits. How much longer they can keep it up one can only guess. I don't think they can do it much longer, as not one of these advances is now yielding them any strategic benefit, and the asset of a talking point to be given out by the German Press Bureau probably does not impress them as a sufficiently good reason to keep taking these losses and making these sacrifices.

Leaving the position we returned to our base, where we spent the night preparatory to moving on the next day to the army that lies next in the line north of us, being the third from the extreme Russian left. My impressions of the condition and spirit of the army visited this day were very satisfactory, and I felt as I did about its southern neighbor—that its movements for the moment have not a vast importance. It may go back now, but when the conditions which are necessary are fulfilled it can almost certainly advance. Probably we need expect nothing important for some months here and further retirements may be viewed with equanimity by the Allies. Not too far away there is a final line which they will not leave without a definite stand and from which I question if they can be driven at all.

CHAPTER XXI
A VISIT TO AN HISTORIC ARMY

BRODY, GALICIA,
July 7, 1915.

FOR the next three days I was with the head-quarters and army of one of the most remarkable fighting organizations that this war has produced on any Front. I am not supposed to mention its number, but I dare say the censor will let me say that it is that one which has been commanded for nearly a year now by General Brussilov. This army, as the reader who has followed the war with any closeness will remember, is the one that entered Galicia from the extreme east in the first week of the war, and that in thirty days of continuous fighting, with practically no rail transport, turned the Austrian right and forced the evacuation of Lwow at the end of August. In spite of their losses and exhaustion this army marched right on the re-inforced Austrian centre and engaged that force with such ferocity, that when the position of Rawa Ruska fell the Grodek line collapsed before its attacks. Still unexhausted and with practically no rest, the same troops, or what was left of them, plus reinforcements, moved on Przemysl, and by their fierce assaults laid the foundation for what subsequently became the siege of the Austrian stronghold. But Brussilov was no man to cool his heels on siege operations, and when the investment was completed, his corps swept on past, and began driving the Austrians back toward the Carpathians.

As the New Year came, and the weeks passed by, the whole world watched his devoted troops forcing back the Austrians and their newly arrived German supports back into the passes which had been considered all but impregnable. He was well through the Dukla and making headway slowly but surely when the great German blow fell on the Dunajec. Leaving his successful operations in the Carpathians, he fell back rapidly in time to connect with the retreating army of the Dunajec and temporarily brace it up for its temporary stand on the San. The defence of Przemysl fell to the lot of the General, but as he himself said to me, "There was nothing but a heap of ruins where had been forts. How could we defend it?" Still, they did defend it for as many days as it took the enemy to force the centre, which had not sufficient forces to stem the advancing tide that was still concentrated against them. Even then, as I am assured by a Staff officer, they hung on until their right flank division was uncovered and menaced with envelopment, when once more they were obliged to withdraw in the direction of the city of Lwow.

After the Russian evacuation of Lwow. The Bug Lancers retreating in good order.

In this retreat there is no denying that the devoted army was hammered heavily, and probably its right flank was somewhat tumbled up in the confusion. Nevertheless, it was still full of fight when the Grodek line was reached. By this time, however, the greater strategy had decided on retiring entirely from Galicia, or very nearly so, to a point which had already been selected; and the battle on the Grodek line was a check rather than a final stand, though there is no question that the Russians would have stopped had the rest of their line been able to hold its positions. But the shattered army of the Dunajec, in spite of reinforcements, was too badly shaken up, and short of everything, to make feasible any permanent new alignment of the position. The action around Lwow was not a serious one, though it was a hard fought and costly battle. It was made with no expectation of saving the town, but only to delay the Germans while other parts of the line were executing what the Russians call "their manœuvres."

From Lwow to the position where I found the army, was a rearguard action and nothing more, and apparently not a very serious one at that. The best authorities have told me that the Russians withdrew from Lwow city in a perfectly orderly manner, and that there was neither excitement nor confusion, a state of affairs in great contrast to that which existed when the Austrians left in September. The Austrian staff took wing in such hot haste that the General's maps, with pencils, magnifying glasses and notes were found lying on the table just as he had left them when he hurried from the room. The Russians may also have panic on occasions, but if they have I certainly have never seen any indication of it in any of the operations that I have witnessed.

The new line occupied runs from approximately the head of the Zota Lipa along the Bug in the direction of Krasne, where the Austrians hold the village and the Russians the railroad station, and thence in the general direction of Kamioka and slightly west of Sokal where the army which lies between it and the former army of the Dunajec begins. In going over this terrain, I was of the opinion that this line was not designed originally as the permanent stand; but the removal of German troops from this Front has sufficiently weakened the Austrians, so it is quite possible that it may become the low water mark of the retreat. However, it is of very little importance, in my opinion, whether the army holds on here, or continues to retreat for another 60 or 80 versts, where prepared positions at many points give excellent defensive opportunities. This army as I found it is in good shape. It is true that many of its corps have been depleted but these are rapidly filling up again. There is reason to believe, however, that this army is no longer the objective of the enemy, and that for the present at least it will not be the object of any serious attack. Behind it for many versts there is nothing of sufficient strategic importance the capture of which would justify the enemy in the expenditure which will be necessary to dislodge it.

I met General Brussilov several times and dined with him the first evening after spending almost three-quarters of an hour with him looking at the maps of the position. I think it would be impossible for anyone to be a pessimist after an hour with this officer. He is a thin-faced handsome man of about fifty-five; in every respect the typical hard-fighting cavalry officer. He is just the man one would expect to find in command of an army with the record that his has made. I asked him if he was tired after his year of warfare. He laughed derisively. "Tired! I should say not. It is my profession. I shall never be tired." I cannot of course quote him on any military utterances, but I left him with the certainty that he at least was neither depressed nor discouraged. That he was disappointed at having to retire is certainly true; but it is with him as I have found it with many others—this set-back has made them only the more ardent for conditions to be such that they can have another try at it and begin all over again. All these ranking officers have unlimited faith in the staying qualities of their men, and little faith in what the Austrians will do when the Germans go away. If *moral*, as Napoleon says, is three times the value of physical assets we need have no fear as to the future where Brussilov is in command of an army.

The General at once agreed to let me visit some observation point where I could have a glimpse of his positions and the general nature of the terrain. On his large scale map we found a point that towered more than 200 metres above the surrounding country, and he advised me to go there. So on the following day we motored to a certain army head-quarters, where the General in command gave us one of his staff, who spoke English, and an extra motor, and sent us on our way to a division then holding one of the front line trenches. Here by a circuitous route, to avoid shell fire, we proceeded to the observation point in question. It was one of the most beautifully arranged that I have ever visited, with approaches cut in through the back, and into trenches and bomb-proofs on the outside of the hill where were erected the hyperscopes for the artillery officers to study the terrain.

I could clearly see the back of our own trenches with the soldiers moving about in them. In the near foreground almost at our feet was one of our own batteries carefully tucked away in a little dip in the ground, and beautifully masked from the observing eye of the aeroplanist. To the south lay the line of the Austrian trenches, and behind that a bit of wood in which, according to the General who accompanied us, the Austrians had a light battery hidden away. Still further off behind some buildings was the position of the Austrian big guns, and the artillery officer in command of the brigade, whose observation point was here, told me that there were two 12-inch guns at this point, though they had not yet come into action.

Directly east of us lay the valley of the Bug, as flat as a board, with the whole floor covered with areas of growing crops, some more advanced in ripeness than others, giving the appearance from our elevation of a gigantic chessboard. Away off to the west some big guns were firing occasionally, the sound of their reports and the bursting shells drifting back lazily to us. At one point on the horizon a village was burning, great clouds of dense smoke rolling up against the skyline. Otherwise the afternoon sunshine beat down on a valley that looked like a veritable farmer's paradise, steeped in serenity and peace. For an hour we remained in this lovely spot, studying every detail of the landscape, and wondering when if ever it would be turned into a small hell of fury by the troops that now lay hidden under our very eyes. We left shortly before six and motored back in the setting sunlight to our head-quarters. Early the next morning I again went to see General Brussilov and almost the first thing he told me was that there had been a stiff fight the night before. The reader may imagine my disappointment to learn that within two hours of my departure the Austrians had launched an attack on the very chessboard that I had been admiring so much during the afternoon in the observation station. From this point, in comparative safety, I could have watched the whole enterprise from start to finish with the maximum of clearness and the minimum of risk. I have never seen a more ideal spot from which to see a fight, and probably will never again have such an opportunity as the one I missed last night.

I heard here, as I have been hearing now for a week, that there was a tendency for the Germans to disappear from this Front, and it was believed that all the troops that could be safely withdrawn were being sent in the direction of Cholm-Lublin, where it was generally supposed the next German drive against the Russians would take place. At the moment this point on the Russian Front represented the serious sector of their line, and so we determined not to waste more time here but to head directly for Cholm and from there proceed to the army defending that position, the reformed army of the Dunajec. Leaving that afternoon we motored back into Russia, where the roads are good, and headed for Cholm. On the way up I called at the head-quarters of the army lying between Brussilov and the army of the Dunajec (as I shall still call it for identification), where I lunched with the General in command and talked with him about the situation. He freely offered me every facility to visit his lines, but as they were far distant and the only communications were over execrable roads which were practically impossible for a motor, and as his Front was not then active, it did not seem worth while to linger when there was prospect of a more serious Front just beyond. As I am now approaching the zone which promises to be of interest in the near future, it is necessary for me to speak of positions and armies with some ambiguity if I am to remain in the good graces of the censor. Suffice to say that the army I skipped holds a line running from the general direction of Sokal, along the Bug to the vicinity of Grubeschow, where it bends to the west, hitting into a rough and rolling country, with its flank near a certain point not too far south-east of Cholm.

I cannot speak authoritatively of this army as I did not visit the positions, though I know of them from the maps. I believe from the organizations attached to it, some of which I know of from past performances, that this army is perfectly capable of holding its own position as it now stands, providing strategy in which it is not personally involved does not necessitate its shifting front. If its neighbour on the west should be able to advance, I dare say that this army also might make some sort of a move forward.

It is futile at this time to make any further speculation. Even at best my judgments in view of the length of front and shortness of time at my disposal must be made on extremely hurried and somewhat superficial observation. It may be better, however, to get a somewhat vague idea of the whole front than to get exact and accurate information from one army, which in the final analysis may prove to be an inactive one in which no one is interested.

CHAPTER XXII
THE NEW ARMY OF THE FORMER DUNAJEC LINE

CHOLM,
July 11, 1915.

EVER since I started up the line of armies from the Bukovina, I have been apprehensive about the point in the line held by this army which suffered so badly on its old position when it was the object and centre of the great German drive in Galicia. The position which it occupies from a point perhaps forty odd versts south-east of Cholm, through a point somewhat south of Krasnystav to the general direction of Bychawa, is at present the most serious point of German advance. It is clear that the capture of Lublin with its number of railroads centring there, would paralyse the position of the whole line. As I have said before, this stroke doubtless represents the one that the enemy most gladly would accomplish in their whole Galician movement, for the pressing of the Russians back here would probably spell the evacuation of Warsaw, an object for which the Germans have spent so many hundreds of thousands of lives, so far to no purpose.

As I have crossed a number of the recuperating fragments of the old Dunajec army in quarters where they were having comparatively an easy time, I was curious to see how the new one was composed. I was received kindly by the General in command, and soon realized that his army, save in number, was practically an entirely new organization built up from corps that have been taken from all quarters of the Russian Front for this purpose. The General himself is new to the command, and so one may regard this organization quite apart from the history of the one that bore the burden of the great Galician drive in May. As soon as I saw the corps here, I came to the conclusion at once that the Russians had reached a point where they intended to make a serious fight. I at once recognized four corps which I have known in other quarters of the war, and wherever they have been they have made a reputation for themselves. The sight of these magnificent troops pouring in made one feel that whether the battle, which every one seems to think is impending, should be won or lost, it would be an action of the most important nature. The new General impressed me as much as any soldier I have seen in Russia. Heretofore he has been in command of a corps which is said to be one of the finest in the whole Russian Army. I had never seen him until this visit, and as a matter of fact I had never even heard of his name. When he came into the room with his old uniform blouse open he was a picture of a rough-and-ready soldier. Steel blue eyes under heavy grey brows and a great white moustache gave an impression of determination, relieved by the gentleness that flickered in the blue of his eyes as well as the suggestion of sensitiveness about the corners of his firm mouth. From the first sentence he spoke, I realized that he meant business, and that this army, when the time came and whatever the results might be, would put up a historic fight.

A Russian eight-inch gun going into position during the fighting round Lublin.

At his invitation I went with him later in the afternoon to look at some new guns that had just come in. They were very interesting and encouraging, but cannot be discussed at present. With them had come new artillerymen, and the general went about addressing each batch. His talk was something like this, freely translated, "Welcome to my command, my good children. You are looking fit and well, and I am glad to have you with me. Now I suppose that you think you have come here to help me hold back the Germans. Well, you are mistaken. We are not here to hold anybody, but to lick the enemy out of his boots, and drive them all clean out of Russia, Poland and Galicia too, and you look to me like the men that could do the job." The Russian soldiers usually cheer to order, but these soldiers responded with a roar, and when dismissed ran off to their positions cheering as long as they could be seen.

That night I dined with the General. In the midst of dinner some reinforcements passed up the street weary and footsore from a long day on the road. The General, dragging his staff with him, went out into the street, and stood, napkin in hand, watching each company as it passed him and calling to each a word of greeting. As the men passed one could see that each was sizing up the chief in whose hands rested their lives, and the future of their army; one could read their thoughts plainly enough. "Here is a man to trust. He will pull us through or die in the attempt."

After dinner I went for a stroll with him, and he did not pass a soldier without stopping to speak for a moment. Late in the evening I saw him walking down the main street of the primitive little town stick in hand, and at every corner he stopped to talk with his men. I have never seen an army where the relations between officers and men were as they are in Russia, and even in Russia not such as between this man and his own soldiers. Already he has lost his own son in the war, yet has accepted his loss with a stoicism that reminds one a little of General Nogi under similar circumstances. This then is the man to whom Russia has entrusted what for the moment appears as her most important front.

The General permitted Prince Mischersky to accompany me during my visit to the positions on the following day. The Prince who is the personal aide-de-camp of the Emperor, and a charming man, took me in his own motor, and early we arrived at the head-quarters of a certain army corps. From here we drove to the town of Krasnystav where was the General of a lesser command. This point, though 14 versts from the German gun positions, was under fire from heavy artillery, and two 8-inch shells fell in the town as we entered, spouting bricks and mortar in every direction while great columns of black smoke poured from the houses that had been struck. While we were talking with the General in his rooms, another shell fell outside with a heavy detonation. From here we visited the division of another corps, where we borrowed horses and rode up to their reserve trenches and had a look at the troops, some of the most famous in Russia, whose name is well known wherever the readers have followed the fortunes of the war. We were perhaps 600 or 800 yards from the front line, and while we chatted with the grizzled old commander of a certain regiment, the enemy began a spasm of firing on the front line trench ahead of us, eleven shells bursting in a few minutes. Then they suspended entirely and once again quiet reigned through the woodland in which our reserves were.

From here by a narrow path we struck off to the west and worked our way up into one of the new front line trenches which are laid out on an entirely new plan, and have been in course of preparation ever since the days of the fighting on the San. They are the best trenches I have ever seen, and are considerably better in my opinion than those on the Blonie line in front of Warsaw which, before this, were the best that had ever come under my observation. Many things that I saw during this day led me to the conclusion that the Russians were doing everything in their power to prevent a repetition of the drive on the Dunajec. The German line of communications here, as I am informed, runs viâ Rawa Ruska, and owing to the difficulties of the terrain between where they now stand and the Galician frontier, it will be very difficult for them to retire directly south. Success in an action here, then, is of great importance to them. If they attack and fail to advance, they must count on the instant depression of the whole Austrian line, for the Austrians even when successful have not been greatly enthusiastic. If they are driven back, they must retire in the direction of Rawa Ruska, across the face of the army standing to the east; they must strike west through Poland, crossing the front of the army lying beside the Vistula; or they must try to negotiate the bad roads south of them, which present no simple problem. If the Russian centre can give them a good decisive blow there is every reason to believe that both flanking armies can participate pretty vigorously in an offensive. No one attaches much importance to the Austrians if the Germans can be beaten. As long as they continue successful, the Austrians, however, are an important and dangerous part of the Russian problem.

Russian artillery officers in an observation position during the fighting round Lublin.

CHAPTER XXIII
BACK TO THE WARSAW FRONT

Dated:
WARSAW,
July 24, 1915.

LEAVING Lublin early in the morning we motored to that certain place where the army next in line to the one I have last discussed is stationed. Since I have been away there have been many changes and much shifting about of corps, and I find that nearly half of this army is now east of the Vistula, and its left joins the right of the one we have just left, the two together forming the line of defence on Lublin. As I have been in the army on the Vistula two or three times before, I find many friends there, and learn from them of the successful movement of a few days before when an early Austrian advance taken in the flank resulted in a loss to the enemy, of prisoners alone, of 297 officers and a number reported to be 23,000 men, practically all of whom are said to be Austrians. Here as elsewhere great confidence is expressed as to the position in the south. We are even told that the bulk of the Germans are now being shifted to another point, and that the next blow will fall directly on or north of Warsaw.

On returning to Warsaw I found that during our absence there had been a grave panic caused by the advances in the south, and that several hundred thousand of the population had already left, while practically all the better class had departed a week ago. The hotels were almost deserted, and the streets emptier than I have ever seen them. But friends who are unusually well informed told me that the danger was past, and the general impression was that the worst was over on this front. For two whole days we had a period practically without rumours or alarms, and then began what now looks to be one of the darkest periods that any of us have yet seen here, not even excepting the panicky days of October last when the Germans were all but in the city itself. First came rumours of heavy fighting to the north, around Przasnys, Lomza, Ciechanow, and reports of Russian reverses and retirements on a new line of defence, and forthwith Warsaw was again thrown into a state of excessive nerves. One becomes so accustomed to these constant alarms that they have come to make little impression on one. The next day a friend coming in from the armies engaged announced with the greatest confidence that the situation was better, and that the new Russian line was in every way better than the old one and that everything was going well. Fighting which is reported to be serious is going on to the south of us, on the Lublin-Cholm line, but is not causing serious anxiety here. On the whole nearly all the usually well-informed persons here felt moderately easy about the situation.

Retreat from Warsaw. Burning crops.

The retreat from Warsaw. A Jewish family leaving Warsaw.

Suddenly there came a bolt out of the blue. With no warning it was announced that the evacuation of Warsaw had been ordered and that the civil authorities would leave on Sunday, July 18. This announcement was not made until late on Saturday, and immediately began the tumult of reports of disaster which we who have sat here through thick and thin know so well. Personally I should have felt no anxiety, for there seemed no immediate danger on any of the near-by fronts, nor serious reverses as far as was known here on the more distant fronts; but the order of evacuation was followed up at once by instructions to the Consul of Great Britain to be prepared to leave on Monday, while I believe that the Belgian and French Consuls received similar notices and are all departing on that day (to-morrow, July 19). The American Consul, Hernando Desote, who already has the German and Austrian interests in charge, took over the British interests at twelve o'clock to-day, and will probably do the same for the interests of the other Allies represented here in Warsaw.

In the meantime we hear that the Russians are falling back on the Blonie line, and that Zuradov has already been evacuated, which may or may not be true. It now seems quite obvious that something has taken place of which we know nothing, and I have not seen or talked with an officer who thinks that what is taking place is due to the local military situation as far as it is known. The general opinion is that if the Russians retire it is due purely to the fact that they have not the munitions to maintain a sustained attack of the Germans who seem to be coming over to this front in increasingly large numbers. For the observer here it is impossible to know what the Russians have in their caissons. One who gets about a good deal can make a guess at the positions, strength and morale of an army, but the matter of munitions or outside policy is something which cannot be solved by the man at the front. There is undoubtedly a feeling of great discouragement here at present, and many believe that the Russians have been bearing the burden now ever since January, while the Allies for one cause or another have not been able to start enough of an attack in the west to prevent the Germans from sending more and ever more troops over here.

Retreat from Warsaw. A Polish Jew. Note his belongings tied round a cow's neck.

Russia certainly has neither the industrial system nor the industrial temperament to supply herself with what she needs to the same extent as both France and England. She has been fighting now for months, with ammunition when she had it, and practically without it when it failed her. Month after month she has kept up the unequal struggle, and there are many here who think the greater powers that be are going to withdraw to a shorter line, and await refilling of their caissons until the time comes when the Allies can co-operate in the attack on the common enemy. These matters are purely speculation, however, for here we know nothing except that the civil evacuation is going on apace, and that there are many signs which indicate that it may be followed by the military within a week or ten days.

The Poles are utterly discouraged, the Russians disgusted and, all things considered, Warsaw at the present writing is a very poor place for an optimist. We hear to-day that the fire brigade has come back from Zuradov, where buildings which might be of use to the enemy are said to have been blown up. Poles have been notified that the Russian Government would give them free transportation from here, and 14 roubles. Factories which have copper in their equipment have been dismantled, and many are already in process of being loaded on to cars for shipment to Russia proper. I am told that the State Bank left yesterday for Moscow, and that they are collecting all the brass and copper utensils from the building next door to the hotel. My chauffeur has just come in and lugubriously announced that benzine has risen to 15 roubles a pood (I do not know how that figures out in English equivalent except that it is prohibitory), when we usually pay three. In addition the soldiers are collecting all private stocks, and there are few of the privately owned cars in the town that have enough in their tanks to turn a wheel with. In the meantime another man informs me that they are tearing down copper telephone and telegraph wires to points outside of the city, and that our troops are already falling back on Warsaw. All of this is very annoying to one who has just finished writing an optimistic story about the situation in the South.

Something like this, then, is the situation in Warsaw on Sunday night, July 18. It has never been worse so far as I can judge from my point of view, but I am of the opinion that things are not as bad as they look, and that successes in the South may yet relieve the tension.

The evacuation of Warsaw. Copper and bells were all taken away before the Russians left.

The retreat from Warsaw.

CHAPTER XXIV
THE LOSS OF WARSAW

Dated:
Petrograd,
August 15, 1915.

THE giving up of Warsaw marks the end of a definite period in the war, and represents the climax of one of the most remarkable campaigns in the history of the world. Military records do not present anything even approaching the effort which in three months has been made by the enemy. From the moment they began their attack on the Dunajec line in early May, until their entrance into Warsaw, almost exactly three months later, their campaign has represented one continuous attack. Every detail seems to have been arranged, and once the movement started, men and munitions were fed into the maw of war without intermission until their objective, Warsaw, was attained. All of this one must in justice accord the Germans, for it is their due. The determination and bravery of their soldiers in these three months of ghastly sacrifice have never faltered.

Their objective has been attained; but when we have said this, our admiration for a purpose fulfilled stops short. Though obtaining Warsaw they have not secured the results that they believed Warsaw represented; and I believe it perfectly safe to say that the capture of Warsaw, without the inflicting of a crashing blow to the Russian Army, was perhaps the greatest disappointment to the Germans which this war has brought them. I know from conversations with many prisoners, that generally speaking, every soldier in the German Army on this Front felt that with the capture of the great Polish capital, the war with Russia was practically finished. It was because this was so earnestly believed that it was possible to keep driving the soldiers on and on, regardless of life and of their physical exhaustion.

The German plan involved the destruction of the army. They have the husk of victory, while the kernel, as has happened many times before in this war, has slipped from their grasp. Everything that has happened since Warsaw is in the nature of a secondary campaign, and really represents an entirely new programme and probably a new objective or series of objectives. From the wider point of view, the war against Russia has begun all over again, and for the present it seems unwise to discuss or prophesy the outcome of the vast operations which have taken place since August 5. But it is a desperate new undertaking for Germany to enter upon after her incomparable exertions these last three months.

The retreat from Warsaw. Ammunition on the road.

In dealing with such extended operations at this time, it is impossible to write accurately, because the Front has been so great that nine-tenths of the information in regard to details is not yet available. The writer was for the period from July 10 to August 5 in daily contact with this Front, and in that period motored thousands of versts, was in practically all of the armies involved in what may be called the Warsaw movement, and at the positions in innumerable places. Yet he hesitates to attempt to write anything of an authoritative nature for the moment, although he believes the rough outline which follows will prove approximately accurate when the history of the movement is written from the broader perspective which time only can bring.

It was the opinion of many observers early in May, including the writer, that Warsaw was the main objective of the great Galician drive. The Germans intended first to strengthen the *moral* of the Austrians by returning them Galicia, but probably the greatest value of the capture of Galicia was the position which left the Germans on the flank of Warsaw. Since last Autumn it has been clear that the Germans regarded Warsaw as the most important strategic prize on this Front, and those who have followed the war will recall the constant series of attacks on the Polish capital. First came their direct advance which frittered away the middle of December, and left them sticking in the mud and snow on the Bzura line in Poland, still 50 versts from their prize. Spasmodic fighting continued until January, when their great Bolimov drive was undertaken. Beginning in the last days of January it continued for six consecutive days. We are told that ten divisions backed by 600 guns attacked practically without interruption for six days and six nights. I cannot accurately state what the German losses were, but I know the Russians estimated them to be 100,000.

It was clear that Warsaw was not to be taken from the front, and as the last gun was being fired on the Bolimov position, the new Prussian flanking movement was launched in East Prussia. This, though scoring heavily in its early days, soon dissipated as the Russians adjusted themselves to the shock. That was followed instantly by another series of operations directed against Warsaw from the North. This too went up in smoke, and for several weeks there was a lull, interrupted here and there by preliminary punches in different parts of the line, intended to discover weakness which did not appear. By April it was clear that Warsaw was not vulnerable from the front or North. Then followed the great Galician campaign which ended with the fall of Lemberg, and by the end of June left the Germans in their new position with the southern flank of the armies in Poland prepared for their final drive for Warsaw on the South. From the light which I have on this campaign I will try and give the sketch as it has appeared to me.

During the retreat from Warsaw.

Russian armoured motor-car.

There is no question that the German strategy aimed not merely at the capture of Warsaw, but at the destruction or capture of the greater part of the army defending the Polish capital. The German programme was carefully prepared, and this time they had no isolated movements, but two great movements developing simultaneously; one aimed to cut the Warsaw-Petrograd lines from the North, and the other aimed at Warsaw from the South. The time which has elapsed is not sufficient, nor is the information available, to enable one to judge at this time whether the Northern or Southern movement was the main German objective. I was in the Cholm-Lublin Army head-quarters just before the heavy fighting began, and was then of the opinion that the most important German activity was contemplated on this sector. It is apparent by a glance at the map, that an overwhelming success here would have been of incredible importance to the enemy. Had they been able to destroy this army as they did the one bearing the same number on the Dunajec in May, they could have moved directly on Brest-Litowsk by Wlodava and cut the Warsaw line of communications to the direct rear 180 versts away. A rapid success here would have certainly resulted in just the disaster that the Germans were hoping would be the outcome of their programme.

The movement on the North from the direction of Mlawa toward Przasnys-Ciechanow was of course a direct threat on the Warsaw-Petrograd line of communications. Success here would have forced the evacuation of the city and a general change of the Russian line; but even had it been a sweeping one, it had not the potentialities of the calamity which a similar success on the Cholm line would have had. Perhaps the Germans estimated both to be of approximately equal importance, and a double success, occurring simultaneously, would have undoubtedly repeated the Moukden fiasco on an infinitely larger scale. It must be remembered that when this movement started, the Russians in the South were at the end of a gruelling campaign of nearly two months' continuous warfare, in which, through lack of munitions, they were obliged to withdraw under difficult and extremely delicate circumstances. The army defending the Cholm-Lublin line was in name the same that had been so very badly cut up six weeks earlier, and the Germans no doubt believed that every one of the Russian Armies engaged from the Bukowina to the Vistula had been so badly shaken up that any effective resistance would be impossible. It was because their estimate was so far out that their programme was doomed to disappointment.

The retreat from Warsaw. Wounded in a barn outside Warsaw.

My own observation of the Russian Armies is that if they are given a fortnight, or even a week, in which to recuperate, they are good for a month of continuous fighting. With almost any other army in the world, after such an experience as the Russians had had for six weeks in Galicia, the defence on the Cholm-Lublin line would have failed, and the Germans might well have driven through to Brest in two or three weeks, as they no doubt firmly believed that they would. But the Russians on the Cholm-Lublin line had the benefit of interior lines of communications, and had also the brief breathing space which enabled them to pull themselves together. Besides this, a new General, General Loesche, was in command, and with him were an important number of the best corps in the Russian Army. Excellent field works had been prepared, and personally, after visiting the positions I felt sure that whatever the outcome of the German move against him might be, it would not result in anything like the Dunajec enterprise, nor would the enemy be able to drive through to Brest with sufficient rapidity to cut off the retreat of the Warsaw army or those lying south of it. The movement in the South started with such terrific impetus, that for several days it seemed possible that in spite of the stamina and leadership of the Russians the enemy would have their way; but after ten days of fighting it became clear that though the enemy were advancing, their progress was going to be of so slow and arduous a nature that they would never be able to inflict a smashing disaster on the Russian Armies.

The details of the battles that raged here for weeks would fill a volume. Although I visited this army several times during this stage, and was in four different corps on this Front, I have still but the vaguest outline in my own mind of the fighting except as a whole. Every day there was something raging on some part of the line, first in one place and then in another. The Germans used the same practice that was so successful in Galicia and massed their batteries heavily. This method, backed by the Prussian Guards, enabled them to take Krasnystav. The best trenches that I have ever seen in field operations were washed away in a day by a torrent of big shells. The Russians did not retreat. They remained and died, and the Germans simply marched through the hole in the line, making a change of front necessary.

The retreat from Warsaw. German prisoners housed in a barn. Note the Russian soldiers have German rifles.

But this time there was no disorganization of the line as a whole. The moment the Germans were beyond their supporting artillery, the Russian infantry were at their throats with the bayonet and drove them back. The fighting from day to day for weeks was a great zig-zag, with German advances and retreats before Russian counter-attacks. But each advance left the enemy a little nearer their objective, and it was clear that slowly but surely they were, by superior forces, vastly superior supplies of ammunition and a constant flow of reserves, forcing the Russians back toward the Lublin-Cholm-Kovel line of railroad. It became equally obvious however after ten days that they would never reach Brest in time to menace seriously the future of the Warsaw army, even if they could and would spare the men to turn the trick.

As a fact it became apparent here for almost the first time, that the Germans in spite of their anxiety to attain their objective, were endeavouring to spare their troops. For the first time I heard the general comment among officers, that the artillery was now the main arm in modern warfare, and the infantry its support. I think this potential failure of their programme dawned on the Germans even before it did on the Russians; for while all eyes were still on the Southern Front, the Germans were reinforcing and pushing their Northern attack which aimed to hit through Pultusk and Wyszkow to the Petrograd-Warsaw line at Lochow. Perhaps after the first two weeks in the South this really was their greatest aim. Personally I think their chance for inflicting a disaster slipped when they failed to defeat definitely, or destroy the army of Loesche. To him and to the left flanking corps of Evert, must be accorded the credit of saving this sector with all its menaces to the future of the campaign and perhaps the whole European situation. For the last two weeks before the abandonment of Warsaw, these two great battles, one in the North and one in the South, were raging simultaneously.

I left Cholm for the last time on July 22, feeling that the fate of Warsaw would not be decided from that quarter, and, for the balance of the campaign, divided my time between the South Vistula armies and those defending the Narew line. It now became clear that the great menace lay from the Northern blow, and here we have a very similar story to that of the Southern army. With terrific drives the enemy took Przasnys, Ciechanow, Makow and at last Pultusk, and finally succeeded in getting across the Narew with ten divisions of excellent troops. On this Front, to the best of my judgment, the Germans at this time had 131 battalions of their very best available troops and perhaps fifteen reserve battalions with their usual heavy artillery support. When the crossing of the Narew was accomplished it seemed inevitable that Warsaw must fall and immediately the civil evacuation of the city began.

The retreat from Warsaw. Artillery on the road.

It seemed then that the Germans might in a few days drive through to the railroad, and to save the army in Warsaw an immediate evacuation in hot haste would prove imperative. But the Russian Army defending this sector rallied just as their brothers did in the South. The German drive on Wyszkow took them within 4 versts of the town, while the Russian counter-attack threw them back fifteen, with heavy losses in casualties and prisoners. Then there began here the same sort of slow stubborn fighting that for weeks had been progressing in the South; only here the German advances were slower, and the attainment of their objective less certain. About the same time (July 25-26) the Germans made a try on the Warsaw line itself, but failed miserably, and abandoned any serious effort against the new Blonie line to which the Russians, in order to get the most out of their men and to shorten their line, had withdrawn. It must never be forgotten that the Russian Front was 1,200 miles long, and the inability to supply it with men and munitions had made it necessary to shorten their Front to get the best results from their numbers. It is hard to say what numbers both belligerents had, and even if I knew exactly our strength the censor would not pass my statement. I think it safe to say however, that during these days the Austro-German forces outnumbered the Russians by at least 50 per cent., counting effectives only. This shortening left simply Warsaw itself with its Blonie line from Novo-Georgievsk to Gorakalwara in Russian hands west of the Vistula.

By the 27th-28th of July there came a wave of hope, and those who had lost all optimism picked up their courage once more. I know from the very best authority that up to August 1 it was hoped that Warsaw might still be saved, though every preparation was being made for its evacuation. The cause of this burst of optimism was due to the fact that the terrific German blows both North and South were not gaining the headway that had been expected. Besides, the Russians were getting more and more ammunition, and it seemed more than possible that the Germans might fail of their objective if only they did not receive increasing reinforcements. These two great battles North and South, each seeming equally important, had drawn everything that could be spared to either one point or the other. It was clear then that there must be some link in the chain weaker than the others, and the Germans set out to find this.

During the retreat from Warsaw. Note wounded man.

Without weakening for a moment their attacks on their main objectives, they began (with new reinforcements) to spear about for a point against which to launch still a third attack. Several attempts disclosed the Russians in strength, but at last the enemy discovered that the weakest spot was on the Vistula south of Warsaw. As this was the easiest to defend on account of the river being approximately the line, the Russians had fewer troops and thus the Germans were able to effect a crossing of the river. I am not able to state absolutely the day or the place of crossing, but I am inclined to place it about July 27-28, and I think the first crossing was near the mouth of the Radomika, while I believe another was made about the same date somewhere near the mouth of the Pilica river. The enemy gained an initial advantage at first, but as usual was driven back by a counter-attack, though he still held his position on the East bank of the river.

At this time, as nearly as I can estimate, there were four Russian army corps defending the Blonie line from Novo-Georgievsk to Gorakalwara. With this strength the few sporadic attacks of the Germans were futile. When the first crossing of the Vistula developed, the corps which stood near Gorakalwara crossed the river and countered the northerly crossing, while troops from the neighbouring army to the South, covered the menace on that portion of the line, and it was believed that the enemy had failed here in his objective which it was thought was the Warsaw-Brest line at Nova Minsk. It was believed and probably rightly, that even the three remaining corps on the Blonie line could hold that front, and that the balance had been re-established, for the Russians hoped that the Germans had in their fighting line all the loose formations which were immediately available. About July 30-August 1, the Germans developed three new divisions (believed to have come from France), and these crossed the river, giving them practically two whole corps against half the strength of Russians. It is possible that even these odds might have been overcome by the stubbornness of the Russian soldier, but the Russians learned that three Austrian divisions, said to have come from the Serbian Front were available in immediate support.

The retreat from Warsaw. One of the last regiments to pass through Warsaw.

From this moment it was evident that Warsaw was doomed. To weaken the Front on the Blonie line meant a break there, and re-inforcements could not be sent either from the Narew line or the Southern Front where actions still raged. It was then clearly a mate in a few moves, if the Russians waited for it. But they did not. Instantly began their military evacuation, the cleverness of which must I think be credited to Alexieff and his brilliant Chief of Staff Goulevitch. Those of us who have been studying the Warsaw situation for ten months, imagined that when the evacuation came, if it ever did, it would be through the city. What happened was entirely unexpected. The corps at Gorakalwara slipped over the river on pontoon bridges in the night, supporting the first corps that was already there, effecting the double purpose of getting out of the Warsaw zone, and simultaneously coming in between the Germans and the line of retreat toward Brest. About the same time the corps that lay next to the Vistula, on the Northern end of the Blonie line, slipped out over pontoon bridges and went to support the Narew defenders, thus making impossible the immediate breaking of that line. On August 4, by noon, there was probably not over one corps on the West side of the Vistula. Half of that crossed south of Warsaw before six, and probably the last division left about midnight, and at three a.m. the bridges were blown up. The Germans arrived at six in the morning, which seemed to indicate that they were not even in touch with the Russian rearguard at the end.

What I have written above is to the best of my information the outline of the Warsaw situation, but it may be in details somewhat inaccurate, though I think the main points are correct. In any case there is no question that the whole withdrawal was cleverly accomplished, and in perfect order, and that when the Germans finally closed in, they found an abandoned city. Their reports of having carried Warsaw by storm are undoubtedly true to the extent that they were in contact with some of the last troops to leave. Probably the trenches that they carried by storm were held by a battalion or two of soldiers protecting the rearguard. That the great body had gone long before the Germans know perfectly well, and their claims of having carried the city by assault would, I dare say, bring a smile even to the stolid face of the German soldier.

During all these operations the Germans had at least five shells to the Russians, one, and but for this great superiority they never would have pushed back either the line of the Narew or the Cholm-Lublin line. Russia could not convert her resources into ammunition, and Germany, who for forty years has lived for this day, could. To this fact she owes her capture of Warsaw. The Allies may be assured that Russia stayed until the last minute and the last shell, and then extricated herself from an extremely dangerous position, leaving the enemy to pounce on the empty husk of a city from which had been taken every movable thing of military value. The defence of and final escape from Warsaw is one of the most spectacular and courageous bits of warfare that history presents, and undoubtedly the fair-minded German admits it in his own heart regardless of the published statements of the Staff.

Siberians leaving the last trench before Warsaw.

A batch of German prisoners captured during the retreat from Warsaw.

CHAPTER XXV
CONCLUSION

Dated:

PETROGRAD,
September 2, 1915.

A GREAT deal has happened since the Fall of Warsaw which one must regret, but at the same time the incidents or disasters must be viewed in their proper perspective. The loss of Kovno, Novo-Georgievsk and many other positions are all unfortunate, but must I think be taken as by-products of the loss of Warsaw. With these enormous extended fronts which modern war presents for the same time, there always develop certain points on the line which may be called keystones. In the Galician campaign, the Dunajec line and Gorlice was the keystone. Once this was pulled out and a number of corps eliminated, the whole vast line from the Vistula to the Bukovina was thrown into a state of oscillation. Once the withdrawal of one army started, the whole line, even to the Warsaw Front, was affected. Armies such as the Bukovina army, which was actually advancing for ten days after the first attack began hundreds of miles away, first halted and finally had to come back to maintain the symmetry of the whole. A great Front, changing over hundreds of versts, means that the whole line can stop only when the weakest unit can stop. A chain is no stronger than its weakest link and the same is roughly true of a Front.

We saw this clearly in Galicia. It has been apparent to every one that Warsaw was the keystone of the campaign in Poland. Once Warsaw was given up under the conditions which then existed, everything that has happened could have been foreseen. It was clear to all on this Front who had followed these movements closely, that the next line would be far in the rear, and that when the general change of Front came, many places would have to be sacrificed. Novo-Georgievsk as a matter of course was doomed. Its function was to protect the flank of the Warsaw defences. It actually held out for two weeks after Warsaw was abandoned, and this delay to the Germans enabled the Russians to get their army clear of a dangerously active pursuit. Fortresses in modern war must, as many believe, be regarded as checks to the mobility of an enemy, rather than as permanent blocks to his progress. Noro-Georgievsh was this, and certainly justified the loss of the garrison and the cost of its construction. Liége is a still better example. Certainly no fortress can withstand modern big guns, and if by their sacrifice they play their part in the game, they have more than served their ends. To hold on to a fortress with a large garrison only magnifies its importance, creates a bad moral effect when it falls, and entails the loss of a field army. Perhaps the Austrian conduct of Przemysl will become the historic warning in future wars as what not to do with fortresses. From an extremely intimate contact of the terrain, I felt certain that the next jump from Warsaw would be Brest-Litowsk. I had visited that place five or six times and felt equally sure that if the Germans made a definite bid for it, it would not be defended. The Russians knew this, and in the army there was no keen disappointment at its loss; for I think no one who knew conditions expected that there would be a big battle there, though many believed that the enemy would never try seriously to go further. That they have done so is looked upon by many as a mistake of the Germans. Time only can tell. The Russians are now on the move to another line. The enemy may continue to follow, but in this district one does not see any point the capture of which can have any great benefit which they could ensure before winter sets in. The only result which can seriously assist them is the capture of Petrograd, and even this would not, I believe, insure a peace with Russia.

Refugees on the road to Brest-Litovsk.

As a matter of fact it seems to the writer pretty certain that the enemy will not reach half way to Petrograd before the winter sets in, and after that its capture is increasingly unlikely. Once one has left the Front one obtains more accurate news as to the situation on this line of battle from the foreign papers than from any other source. In Petrograd, in civilian circles, there is great pessimism as to the military situation, but this is not shared by those who are in the confidence of the highest authorities. The only danger that seriously and immediately menaces the Russians is rapidly passing away. It was dangerous because it was insidious. It is certainly worth discussion.

It was of course to be expected that the moment the Russian Armies left Warsaw and the entire line began to retire on new positions, there should be a period of great ambiguity. For several weeks the armies were in constant movement, and from day to day their exact positions were uncertain. As they went back, they obviously left many towns and positions behind them, with the result that for weeks the Germans have been having a continuous celebration over their advances. During this period very little news was available in Petrograd, which at the best is pessimistic and quick to jump at conclusions of disaster. There is here, as all the world knows, an enormous German influence, and whenever the military situation is in the least ambiguous, there start immediately in a thousand different quarters reports of disaster which in an hour are all over Petrograd. That these reports originate from German sympathizers is hardly questioned, and that the whole propaganda is well organized is equally certain.

Roll call during the retreat from Warsaw. All that was left of them.

The past two weeks has found Petrograd in a receptive mood for gloomy news, and inasmuch as nothing of a favourable nature has come from the Russian Army, the German propaganda of insidious and subtle rumours and reports has run through the city like a prairie fire after a drought. Three main themes have been worked up and circulated for all that they would stand. It was said first that there was lack of harmony among the Allies, and that the Russian high authorities were not satisfied with the conduct of the war in the West. The corollary of this of course was that without harmony the cause was lost. Next came the assertion that the army was demoralized, and had lost hope and therefore wanted peace. Then the shortage of ammunition was magnified until half the gullible population were almost willing to believe that the army were fighting with pitchforks and shotguns. Out of all this came the assertion that peace was inevitable and that the Germans would take Petrograd. For a week or more these topics circulated and grew with such alarming rapidity that at last the Government was obliged to take notice of the propaganda, which was finally squelched by a statement issued to *The Times* and the Russian Press by M. Serge Sazonov, the distinguished and clever minister of Foreign Affairs.

In this interview the Russian statesman, speaking for the Government, made a categorical denial of the slanders against the Government and the Russian people. He stated without reservation that there was not now, nor had there ever been, a lack of harmony between the military or civil authorities of the Allies, and announced that the Russian Government not only approved of, but had implicit faith in the programme of the Allies in the West. He then discussed the munitions question, and asserted that all steps were being taken to fill depletions in all branches of the army requirements, and lastly he stated once and for ever that there would be no independent peace with Germany while a single German soldier remained on Russian soil and that the war would continue even if the Government were obliged to retire to the heart of Russia and the contest continued for years to come. This statement has had an immediate effect on the local panic-mongers here, and for the moment there is a lull in the German propaganda.

Resting during the retreat from Warsaw.

In the meantime it is becoming obvious that the Germans in spite of their following up of the retiring Russians are not likely to achieve any successes which can immediately affect the political situation. If they take Riga and Grodno, and even Vilna, they have done their worst for some months to come, and one cannot see what they can accomplish further before winter sets in. If the campaign at this stage were in June one might feel apprehensive of Petrograd, but under the most favourable conditions it is difficult to see how the Germans can get even halfway here before November. By that time they will be on the verge of the winter with the ground freezing so deeply that intrenching is difficult, if not impossible, and every advance must be made with terrific losses. Their attempts to conduct warfare in Poland (a much milder climate) in winter, are too recent a memory to lead one to believe they will repeat it here. It will be remembered that their advance on the Bzura-Rawka line froze up when winter came, and the sacrifice of thousands did not advance them materially at that point in spite of their most determined efforts. I think one may say, then, that what the Germans cannot accomplish before November they will not attempt until Spring. The pessimism and hopelessness of Petrograd seem to be on the wane, and the reports from the Front now arriving do not indicate either demoralization or despair in the army.

Probably one must expect retirements and rearguard actions for some weeks to come. Ultimately the Russians will settle down on some new line from which it is extremely unlikely that they can be driven before the winter sets in. One hesitates to make any prophecies, as conditions change so rapidly that it is always dangerous to do so, but perhaps it is safe to say that with the coming of the winter and the definite lull in the campaign which will follow, the Russians will have passed their crisis. Given four months of rest and recuperation we shall have an entirely new situation in the beginning of next year which will present an entirely new problem. It will really mean the starting of a new war with new objectives and practically with a new and re-equipped army.

There may be those who are disappointed, but history, I believe, will conclude that this summer campaign of the Russians has been the greatest factor so far in the war making for the ultimate victory of the Allies. For nearly four months Germany has been drained of her best. Men and resources have been poured on this Front since May regardless of cost. Autumn approaches with the armies in being, undemoralized and preparing to do it all over again. In the meantime the Allies are preparing to begin on the West, or at least it is generally so believed. When they do at last start, Germany will for months be occupied in protecting herself, and will probably be unable to act so vigorously here. If Russia gets over the period of the next sixty days, she will be safe until Spring, and by that time she will without doubt be able to take up an offensive in her turn.

Wounded returning to Warsaw.

On the banks of the River Dniester. Cossack snipers in the woods overlooking the river.

After months of observation of the Germans it is folly to speculate on how long they can stand this pace. It may be for six months, and it may be for two years, but with the Allies patiently wearing down the enemy month after month and year after year there can be but one end. That Russia has played her part, and played it heroically, I think no one, even the Germans themselves, can deny. There are some that like to believe that the enemy will try to get Moscow and Kiev before winter sets in. The former objective seems impossible, and the latter even if obtained would, I believe, in no way compensate the enemy for his sacrifices, for the nature of the country is such that all advances could only be at terrific cost. Besides, Kiev, even if taken, would not, I think, have any tangible effect on forcing Russia to make peace, and this end alone can justify the Germans in making further huge sacrifices.

There are many who maintain that Russia will find it difficult to reconquer Galicia and Poland. Probably she will never have to do so. It is perfectly possible that when the end comes, Germany will still be on the territory of France, Belgium, and Russia. Peace will bring back instantly all of these provinces without any fighting at all. It matters not, then, whether Germany is broken while still in the heart of Russia or under the walls of Berlin itself.

The task is to break the enemy and that this will be done eventually I think cannot be doubted. It is the stamina, the character and the resources of the Allies that in the end will decide this war, and nothing is more unwise than to judge the situation from the study of pins moved back and forward on the map of Europe.

Milton Keynes UK
Ingram Content Group UK Ltd.
UKHW010742080324
438959UK00004B/327